STATUS QUO **IS NOT** COMPANY POLICY

Heidi Scott

with David A. Naylor

STATUS QUO IS NOT COMPANY POLICY

• • • •

Empowering Innovation
Through Adaptive Leadership

Forbes | Books

Published by Forbes Books, Charleston, South Carolina.
An imprint of Advantage Media Group.

Forbes Books is a registered trademark, and the Forbes Books colophon is a trademark of Forbes Media, LLC.

Printed in the United States of America.

10 9 8 7 6 5 4 3 2 1

ISBN: 979-8-88750-310-3 (Hardcover)
ISBN: 979-8-88750-311-0 (eBook)

Library of Congress Control Number: 2024910778

Cover and layout design by Matthew Morse.

This custom publication is intended to provide accurate information and the opinions of the author in regard to the subject matter covered. It is sold with the understanding that the publisher, Forbes Books, is not engaged in rendering legal, financial, or professional services of any kind. If legal advice or other expert assistance is required, the reader is advised to seek the services of a competent professional.

Since 1917, Forbes has remained steadfast in its mission to serve as the defining voice of entrepreneurial capitalism. Forbes Books, launched in 2016 through a partnership with Advantage Media, furthers that aim by helping business and thought leaders bring their stories, passion, and knowledge to the forefront in custom books. Opinions expressed by Forbes Books authors are their own. To be considered for publication, please visit **books.Forbes.com**.

To my devoted husband, who has been my greatest support and grounding force. And to our wild and barefoot children, whose love, encouragement, and sacrifices have made it possible for me to achieve far more than I ever thought possible. We'll never be ticky-tacky!

To every past and present leader in any capacity. You have faced countless challenges and triumphs in the pursuit of a better tomorrow. Your courage, wisdom, and unwavering commitment to serving others have laid the foundation for generations to come. And to the brave and brilliant leaders of the future, may you draw strength and inspiration from those who have come before you. I hope you always remember that "you become responsible, forever, for what you have tamed" (Antoine de Saint-Exupéry, *The Little Prince*).

May this book serve as a testament to the indomitable human spirit, the power of leadership to transform lives and communities, and the enduring legacy we all have the potential to create.

—HEIDI

• • • •

I firmly believe no one ever rises to a level of any significance on their own. There is always someone in the background or by their side supporting them. My wife, Sarah, is no exception. Someone once told me that Sarah would never allow me to settle. I have spent over thirty years of my life confirming this statement. Thank you.

I'd also be remiss if I didn't say thanks to the many others who I have been fortunate enough to lean on and build on what they had started. John Kirkland hired me and laid a solid foundation, and then the former and current employees of Rayburn truly placed their fingerprints on it. And, without the support and encouragement from the board, none of this would have happened. They are where the rubber meets the road. Rayburn is a special place to me, and I am honored to have been able to invest so much of myself in it.

—DAVID

CONTENTS

FOREWORD

I have had the privilege of working closely with Rayburn Electric Cooperative for the past seven years as an executive coach and advisor. In that time, I have been incredibly impressed by Rayburn's focus on excellence and in their commitment to nurturing a positive workplace culture that fosters business success by recognizing that people are the number one asset. I am also impressed that the Rayburn staff not only believe but are convinced of the importance of their role in the development of this unique culture and in the success of the company.

Status Quo is Not Company Policy: Empowering Innovation Through Adaptive Leadership provides a valuable window into a principle-based culture that thrives on innovation and leadership while keeping a focus on the traditional member-centric cooperative principles that bring vital electricity to those across rural America.

When you walk the hallways of Rayburn, you feel a different energy. You often hear people openly quote CEO David Naylor's mission-based catchphrases and executive-level narratives. This is evidence that the values, goals, and vision of David and his Executive

Team are accepted by staff and cascaded across the culture of the entire organization.

Of all the companies I have worked with in the energy industry as a former executive, regulator, and consultant, Rayburn stands out in the way they do business. They embrace a disruptive, principle-based leadership mindset, one where the key foundational approaches for critical decision-making often pivot away from common business practices to a more creative and flexible way of solving problems. This includes prudently reacting to unexpected changes and quickly regaining their poise when the rush of challenges falls on them.

The true test of leadership is how we respond emotionally and how resilient we are during a crisis. Rayburn's handling of the fallout from the 2021 Winter Storm Uri event speaks volumes about the resilience instilled by the company's emphasis on innovation and creative problem solving. While other companies faltered, Rayburn fostered a sense of well-being in teams during the uncertainty, and they intelligently pursued securitization rather than fold and allow bankruptcy to be the answer.

David Naylor exemplifies the type of forward-thinking, entrepreneurial leader that drives this culture. He strategically interacts with employees, so they understand their role in the company's growth trajectory. He also actively solicits ideas from all team members, not just senior management. This inclusivity spurs innovation and has readied Rayburn to nimbly adapt to industry changes.

As Rayburn has rapidly expanded from a local cooperative to a preeminent national player, it has stayed true to its mission of innovation and of making employees its foremost priority. The stories and insights this book shares will display how investing in people and culture establishes the foundation for sustainable success, no matter the scale or complexity of operations. Rayburn sets an example for organizations of any size or industry to follow.

EARL SHOCKLEY

President and Founder, INPOWERD LLC

Former senior executive at the North American Electric Reliability Cooperation (NERC)

WHAT MAKES RAYBURN, RAYBURN?

BY DAVID A. NAYLOR, CEO, RAYBURN

Sometimes, I find myself contemplating the speed and magnitude of what is now Rayburn. We have become a driven, opportunistic organization that I am truly proud and humbled to be a part of. It is certainly beyond anything I could have imagined or asked for when I joined the organization in 2011 with neither a road map nor detailed goals in mind.

In just the last five-year period, Rayburn grew from $300 million in assets to over $1 billion. We have stared bankruptcy in the face and emerged as the first electric cooperative in the nation to utilize securitization. We stepped into the realm of private equity companies and emerged with the purchase of the 758-megawatt Rayburn Energy Station. Rayburn has grown from just over twenty employees to over eighty employees. And, in our first time participating, Rayburn was named the fifth best small business to work at in the Dallas-Fort Worth metroplex by *The Dallas Morning News* and first for employee benefits. All of this, while providing our Members with more flexibility and opportunities to succeed. Those are accomplishments that most executives would love to see over the span of a career, and I have been incredibly fortunate to watch Rayburn accomplish it all in less than ten years.

So, what makes Rayburn, Rayburn? I admit I look at this with my rose-colored glasses, but here is my viewpoint: Rayburn is Member focused and Member driven. It's not just a tagline or words on a page. As you will see in this book, everything we do is for the user at the end of the line who flips a switch in their living room and deserves to have the light come on every time. In the electricity generation and transmission (G&T) world, it's easy to forget about our distribution cooperative Members in day-to-day operations, but those co-op Members are the reason the lights stay on. Sure, we remember them when we send out the bills and in our board meetings, but because we are essentially the middlemen in the process, it is easy to lose that focus. It is imperative to remember that without our Members, there is no G&T. As we focus on our Members first, Rayburn is changing the way things have always been done in the G&T world.

We continually ask, "What can we do to make our Members successful?" Perhaps, the philosophy of working hard for the success of others comes from my parents teaching me to treat all people with respect. Maybe it comes from my sixteen years of previous consulting experience. Maybe it's just common sense. Regardless, this has been my message and focus from day one. By making our Members more successful, we become more successful. And we do that by looking for new and better ways to accomplish the work.

Innovation truly is one of our core values. For example, we shifted the way we invoice our Members in order to provide them as much flexibility as possible without compromising our financial position or other obligations. This required a different way of thinking, but it really wasn't that hard.

Let's be clear. We can be hyper-focused on our Members' success, but if we don't deliver the goods, then it's all for naught. Which is why Rayburn continually brings in increased expertise. We have made significant efforts to assemble a team of quality employees, top-notch advisors, and trusted counterparties who share our drive and vision. We're not necessarily always focused on cost-effectiveness. In fact, sometimes, we even purposefully avoid the cheapest option because that is the best way to ensure we stay on task and maintain the proper focus. Of course, we consider the bottom line, but as a nonprofit, we are mission-driven, and people are noticing the difference that makes.

It is extremely satisfying to watch as our people embrace and carry out the core values of Integrity, Respect, Excellence, and Innovation. Rayburn is becoming a sought-after mentor to other similar organizations. We are now seeing Rayburn employees serve as experts on panels nationwide. I believe it is a healthy sign of internal success when you see the ripple effect of our mission expanding so far beyond the walls of our offices.

Rayburn is employee-committed. While our Members are our focus, our employees are our soul. I fully subscribe to the theory that if you treat your employees right, they'll reciprocate. We work hard at Rayburn. The accomplishments described here required a lot of manhours, blood, sweat, and tears. Literally, in some cases. Our positions are physically and mentally demanding, yet Rayburn continues to attract top-notch talent. Sure, we have made some mistakes along the way, but we do our best to remedy them quickly and move on. Certainly, our screening process has become a critical tool in our hiring process. We're more interested in the cultural fit than skills or expertise because those can be taught.

Rayburn attempts to meet the employees on three levels:

1. Economic. No matter how good the job is, not many people can afford to work without being paid. Rayburn has worked hard to ensure our salaries and benefits are not only attractive but extremely competitive in the space. Our location near Dallas means we are competing against Fortune 500 companies and others who have far more resources than we do. We are also mindful that, as a nonprofit organization, our costs are borne by those who ultimately pay the electric bill. I want to assure those folks that the value they are getting is phenomenal.

2. Professional. Continual career and personal development is important. At Rayburn, our employees have experienced tremendous opportunities in this regard. Every single employee is given the option to develop in the manner they see best. This is why training is a critical piece of the Rayburn experience. We pay for any relevant certification, professional license, or other learning that an employee needs to succeed in their position. Seems like a small price to pay. Additionally, Rayburn has a tuition reimbursement program where employees can obtain any type of relevant advanced degree and be reimbursed for those costs. As a side note, Rayburn imposes no back-end requirements on the employees for taking advantage of this program. It's Rayburn's responsibility to maintain a culture that makes the employee want to stay as opposed to imposing an obligation on the employee that implies a quid pro quo.

3. Emotional. Employees like to feel they make a difference. Rayburn is involved in our local communities and encourages employees to join us. We have implemented teams across

the organization that help direct those efforts. Rayburn has monthly "Let's Connect" events where employees get together to build camaraderie. These range from crawfish broils to cornhole tournaments to simple ice cream socials. We like to reward folks for their hard work and contributions.

I feel it is important to note that through all of this, there is no entitlement. Employees earn their promotions and raises through their merit and accomplishments. Individuals who believe they are entitled to special recognition or treatment typically don't last long here.

Honest, candid relationships matter to us. Rayburn invests deeply in the trust bank. This single most important strength could arguably also be our biggest weakness—we trust our folks. I mean really trust them. This makes us vulnerable, which can be very uncomfortable. In a perfect world, every single employee would use that trust to the benefit of the company, but on a rare, unfortunate occasion, former employees have exploited that trust. This required swift and decisive action. But instances like this don't stop us from encouraging our people to be emboldened and energized to make a difference.

Everyone here knows that even if mistakes are made, the consequences are focused on learning from mistakes rather than imposing penalties. Staff members understand that the Executive Team fully supports them. Our core value is excellence, not perfection. This becomes a powerful thread when woven within the rest of the Rayburn fabric, and it has helped us achieve what we've accomplished and will achieve in the future.

All of this is what makes Rayburn, Rayburn. We have a commitment to continued improvement because traditional approaches and methods, both internal and external, have shifted and will continue to shift. Every individual contribution of every person in the company has furthered the corporate success we enjoy today.

I feel a deep sense of accomplishment when I look at what we've done and by seeing our people continue to develop and advance. I make no apologies for the steps we've taken because status quo is not company policy, and I can't wait to see what Rayburn becomes.

CHAPTER 1

DARKNESS TO LIGHT

Electricity is not a luxury.

DAVID A. NAYLOR

Who is Thomas Edison?

The guy who invented the light bulb, right?

OK.

And who was Humphry Davy?

Turns out, he was the guy who actually invented the light bulb.

It's true. This British chemist was the first to recognize that an electrical current would jump across gaps in circuits, producing enough electricity to light up a room. It was in 1809, seventy years before Edison's bulb, when Davy connected two charcoal strips to a battery with wires. Light was produced as the current jumped across a gap between the strips, leading him to name it the "arc lamp." This first controllable artificial electric light was the precursor to Edison's incandescent light bulb and to modern lighting today.

Davy was an early disruptor, credited for critical advances in the fields of chemistry, physics, medicine, agriculture, mining, and even photography. As a young man, he loved to wander outdoors and was described as having a quick wit and lively imagination. As he matured, he was always experimenting, with a unique talent for inquiry. Later in life, he was knighted for his significant contributions to the advancement of humankind.

Throughout history and in every industry, changemakers are always those who wander, experiment, and use their imaginations. They dare to question, push boundaries, and ask how things can be made better.

Organizations can be changemakers too. Look at the way Netflix changed entertainment. How Amazon changed shopping. How Google changed access to information. Or how Airbnb changed vacationing. Certainly, these companies were only able to impact the world the way they did because of the talented and visionary people behind the corporate name.

Sitting quietly in northeastern Texas near Dallas is an organization that, like Davy, is disrupting the status quo and pushing boundaries in its industry. Rayburn Electric Cooperative is not your typical utility company. To outsiders, it might look like a basic electric company in a sleepy little town on a lake. But inside its headquarters, it has been quietly making history for decades.

Rayburn is redefining traditional norms and surpassing industry standards. It is playing a proactive role in establishing a fundamental shift in the way electric companies, particularly electric cooperatives, function today. From staff members who create their own job descriptions to executives with Nerf guns on their desks, this not-so-little company in a place few people have heard of is pushing the boundaries of leadership, of what it means to work as a team, and of what a growth mindset can actually do.

In 2021, the company found itself on the brink of bankruptcy, after a devastating winter storm that crippled an entire state. Two years later, Rayburn was a $1B company, having survived and thrived when all odds were stacked against it.

This is the story of what makes Rayburn special. Of why Rayburn does what it does. Of the conditions that exist within its organization that allow it to thrive in crisis. Of how Rayburn has adapted and powered through change to become something greater than it was. And more importantly, how any organization of any size can do the same.

As CEO David Naylor said in the introduction, the successes Rayburn has seen come from an enormous investment in the advancement of people. It's about hiring for talent and attitude, rather than worrying about job titles and org charts. It's about instilling a pride of ownership in every staff member, offering training they actually want, and supporting their needs by eliminating red tape. And it's about generosity, autonomy, and trust that your people will make wise decisions for the benefit of the entire company.

These principles can be replicated in a tiny local company of less than ten people or major corporations of hundreds or even thousands. They are universal and deceptively simple, but when done right, they will create resilience despite the worst circumstances.

HOW IT WORKS

Before we dive into the incredible Rayburn story and examine how they're shaking things up in ways we can all exemplify, it's necessary to take a quick step back and understand how this whole electricity thing works. Many unsung heroes played a part that led up to you being able to plug your phone into the wall and charge it every night.

For over a hundred years, humankind has grappled with the best ways to generate and distribute energy safely and efficiently. Thomas Edison and Nikola Tesla's "War of the Currents" famously brought this problem to the public mindset during the turn of the century, but it was actually an American physicist named William Stanley Jr. who made the most significant contribution to the conveniences in electricity we take for granted today. As Edison and Tesla battled publicly, Stanley was busy quietly developing the world's first practical transformer—the most essential component of our modern electrical power systems. Transformers allow for the efficient transmission of high voltages over long distances, revolutionizing the way electrical power was distributed.

Stanley's transformer, patented in 1886, became the cornerstone of the alternating current (AC) system, which ultimately triumphed over Edison's direct current (DC) system. The transformer's ability to step up voltage for long-distance transmission and then step it down for safe use in homes and businesses was a game changer. It allowed for the creation of large, centralized power plants that could serve entire cities and regions, making electricity more accessible and affordable than ever before. Without Stanley's groundbreaking invention, the widespread adoption of electricity would most definitely have been significantly delayed, and the modern world as we know it would look very different. Today, as we continue to face challenges in energy production and distribution, it is important to remember the crucial role that innovation and collaboration play in finding solutions. Stanley's unobtrusive perseverance led to a transformative breakthrough that few paid attention to at the time and few remember today.

Thanks to Stanley's invention, access to electricity began to spread across the United States. By the 1930s, the nation was in the midst of the Great Depression. Our cities and towns had been hooked up to regional electrical grids, but only 10 percent of American rural farms were receiving electric service.[1] Power companies could not find a cost-effective way to run wires across the hundreds of miles needed to reach remote homesteads.

By then, electricity had become a standard rather than a luxury. President Franklin D. Roosevelt was keenly interested in bringing it to every American, no matter where they lived. He signed an Executive Order creating the Rural Electrification Administration (REA) in 1935, opening the way for rural communities to develop and install their own power supplies. The most logical way to take advantage of the REA was the creation of electric cooperatives.

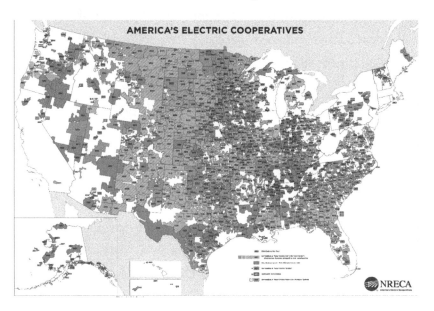

Cooperatives, often referred to as co-ops, are organizations owned and operated by a group of individuals with common interests. Co-ops such as Ocean Spray, True Value, Sunkist, Ace Hardware, and

---

1   Frank Gallant, "Flashbacks: rural electrification by the numbers," December 7, 2016, https://www.cooperative.com/remagazine/articles/Pages/flashbacks-rural-elec-trification-cartogram-numbers.aspx#:~:text=The%20GE%20map%20started%20to,New%20Zealand%20at%2060%20percent.

REI thrive in the corporate world because of their unique model—pooling their resources to achieve common goals. Key features include democratic control, member ownership, and the even distribution of benefits. Profits generated by cooperatives are often reinvested to meet the needs of the members or to further develop the cooperative itself by purchasing goods and services collectively, marketing products in a new way, or providing additional services to members. A distinguishing element is the way co-ops balance economic and social goals while considering the well-being of members as well as the broader communities they serve.

Due to co-op involvement, more than 90 percent of U.S. farms had electricity in less than two decades. Using horse-drawn wagons to move equipment and heavy power poles, early REA-sponsored crews set up power lines using long-handled shovels and pickaxes, and the nation slowly and methodically became a little brighter.

TEXAS CO-OPS

In 1935, United States House of Representatives Speaker Samuel Rayburn sponsored a $33,000 loan to three farmers under the REA. These three farmers contributed $50 each as part of a tiny new electric cooperative they called the Bartlett Community Light & Power Company (BCL&P). The three men ran nearly sixty miles of electric lines out to their small town of Bartlett, Texas, located between Waco and Austin. "In November 1935, BCL&P volunteers and paid employees began setting the first section of 36 poles. Finally, on March 7, 1936, after paying a $5 deposit for an electric meter, Charles Saage was given the big honor: throwing the switch."[2] The lights came on in Bartlett, and the electrification of rural Texas began.

As individual electrical distribution co-ops were formed to bring power to rural residents, the need for wholesale electricity generators and distributors grew, leading to the creation of generation and transmission cooperatives (G&Ts). These wholesalers generate and purchase electricity in bulk and then sell it to local distribution cooperatives, which in turn deliver the power to their member-consumers. Today, Rayburn Electric Cooperative is one of nine G&Ts in Texas.

As the grid grew in Texas due to more farms, homes, and businesses needing power, so did the need for the management of the electric load. This refers to the amount of power being generated and the way that power was sent from where it was generated to the

---

2   Charles Boisseau, "Historic connection," October 2010, https://texascooppower.com/historic-connection/.

places that needed to use it. The solution was to form an independent electric system operator to oversee the scheduling of the more than fifty-two thousand miles of transmission lines and over one thousand generation units (representing about 90 percent of Texas's electric load). The Electric Reliability Council of Texas (ERCOT) was formed as a 501(c)(4) nonprofit corporation to administer these wholesale transactions of power. It is now serving more than twenty-six million customers and is governed by the Texas Public Utility Commission and the Texas Legislature.

As part of this, Rayburn Electric Cooperative manages a 1,200-megawatt system with 90 percent of its end users being residential customers. When it was founded, the company was effectively the middleman between ERCOT and the Member cooperatives who need that power. These Member cooperatives are Fannin Electric Cooperative, Farmers Electric Cooperative, Trinity Valley Electric Cooperative, and Grayson Collin Electric Cooperative, together serving over five hundred thousand Texans across sixteen counties.

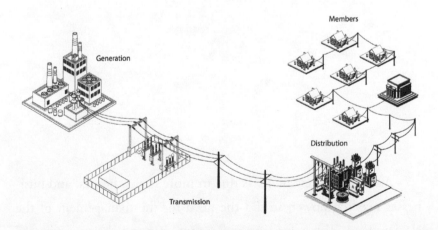

To maintain a constant, dependable supply to all of these people, Rayburn purchases electricity ahead of the demand based on projected needs, so efforts to accurately forecast changes in need is a huge component of this work. Because the entire generation and delivery system is extremely weather-sensitive, temperatures are a key factor in making decisions about these advanced purchases. For example, when the mercury rises, people crank up their air conditioning. When it drops, they kick on the heat. Both of these are predictable, expected patterns that increase electricity demand, and they are accounted for.

The electric industry is a tight-knit community, and it is not uncommon to find second- and third-generation workers who choose a career here. Rayburn Board Chairman David McGinnis exemplifies this as a second-generation G&T employee who has two children now also working for electric cooperatives. These folks band together to plan for and address unpredictable factors like storms, falling branches, aging materials, wildlife damage, and advancements in technology. Just like every good G&T, Rayburn staff communicate closely with their Members and watch conditions closely to determine when they must budget for very large purchases so they can plan accordingly. The worst failure for a G&T is not being able to supply the power that its Members need.

This is a particular focus for G&Ts in the state of Texas, which has always been known for highly affordable electricity in comparison to other states. Cheaper bills combined with a pro-business economic engine have created a highly attractive corporate atmosphere. The relatively low regulatory oversight compared with other states means factories and other businesses continue to flock south. Texas is actively and sometimes even aggressively sought out by industries like cryptocurrency miners that require massive electric loads. Because of this, electric companies must stay on their toes and be ready to pivot as demand changes. But in an industry that can't grow without huge upfront investments before it can upgrade entire infrastructure systems, flexibility is easier said than done.

To keep the lights on, predictability is a good thing wherever you can find it. In the G&T world, it is not generally encouraged (and often even discouraged) to change the way our electrical system works. As you can imagine, this industry is highly regulated because of the very real danger associated with high-voltage currents. A culture of caution has been the industry standard from the very beginning. As Rayburn Board of Directors member John Ed Shinpaugh said, "We were founded by a Congressional Act, so from day one, we had a government handprint on us. We all know that government is all about policy and procedure and guidelines. Because of that, we have grown into a traditional industry that can be very stodgy and immobile."

Fellow Board member Jeff Lane added, "Most electric companies keep doing what everybody else does because it works." Perhaps because of this, disruptors are not commonly found in this industry.

Except Rayburn.

CHAPTER 2

STATUS QUO IS NOT COMPANY POLICY

You must continue casting the vision.

DAVID A. NAYLOR

Electricity equals quality of life. The advent of electric power ushered societies out of darkness and propelled us toward ever-increasing innovation, transformation, and prosperity. Virtually every aspect of life has changed. With the widespread adoption of the electric motor, production rates soared for consumer goods. Concurrently, our increasingly efficient transportation systems continued to develop, sparking a surge in economic growth and international trade. Life-saving medical equipment significantly improved diagnosis, treatment, and patient care. Communication systems were revolutionized. And on a more individual level, because of electricity, it suddenly was less tedious to clean, feed, clothe, shelter, inform, and entertain households the world over. It's probably fair to say electricity changed everything for humanity.

But just as electricity transformed our world, the world itself continues to evolve at an unprecedented pace. Change is not just inevitable; it's normal.

QUESTION EVERYTHING

Economists and social scientists tell us that we live in a VUCA world: volatile, uncertain, complex, and ambiguous. Because of this, change is inescapable.

Research in psychology and organizational behavior suggests that the attitude with which we approach change can significantly influence how successfully we navigate it. Study after study reinforces our understanding that those who approach change with a positive, growth-oriented mindset are better positioned to not only cope with the challenges it presents but also to seize the opportunities it offers for personal development.

Those who resist adjusting or adapting their comfortable state of affairs may think they are ensuring more stability and continuity, but in reality, they are hampering growth and smothering innovation. The main peril for those who resist change is stagnation.

The same can be said for organizations: those that remain open to change thrive while those that resist change often do not.

Every advancement, whether individual or organizational, starts with a creative spirit and a willingness to seek alternative solutions and explore new possibilities. We won't move forward if we can't first challenge the prevailing norms and question assumptions. People who exhibit a willingness to ask questions, seek answers, and then change their approach as needed do not become obsolete or irrelevant. They are the people who are resilient through challenges. As they push their growing edges, they discover higher potential than they ever thought they had, despite the severity of the trial. "Post-traumatic growth" is the phrase used to describe the positive psychological changes some people can experience as a result of struggling with highly challenging life circumstances or traumatic events. Challenging norms doesn't mean we don't recognize limitations, challenges, or weaknesses. Rather, it means we study them for ways to improve ourselves so that when the next one comes, we are better able to face it.

Rayburn Electric Cooperative has the motto "Status Quo is Not Company Policy." While not phrased this exact way until later in the company's history, the sentiment has been one of Rayburn's foundational values from day one. The seed of an idea to form a new company was planted when Ray Raymond, chairman of a group of Texas co-ops, refused to go along with what everyone else was doing. He challenged the status quo when, in the 1970s, the federal Atomic Regulatory Commission (ARC) appeared on the scene. The ARC worked hard to foster overwhelming and eager support from Texas lawmakers, utilities, and municipalities for the construction of a nuclear power plant. Those who opposed the nuclear power proposal were initially in the minority, but after many heated discussions including Raymond as one of the few dissenters, half of the cooperatives favored the plant and half did not.

The two groups split, and in 1979, Rayburn Electric Cooperative was created as the solution for those who did not want to get saddled with the immense debt of a nuclear plant against their will. This decision turned out to be extremely wise, as the power plant costs soared far beyond projections, and those co-ops who had bought in were forced to take legal action to get out of their contractual ties to fund it.

Rayburn was born from a desire to question what felt like the "normal," acceptable thing to do. To resist the status quo.

Just like most start-ups, Rayburn Electric Cooperative initially experienced growing pains. The new Board of Directors and first CEO John Kirkland faced increasingly significant milestones to stay intact. In those early days of Rayburn, there were only five staff members. Husband-and-wife duo John and Annette Kirkland essentially were Rayburn. They had to decide where to get power, what kind of contracts to hold, and what assets the company needed to own. As they built the company from scratch, they did it on the foundation of Integrity, Respect, Excellence, and Innovation. While not official until 2021, these four core values were always the driving force behind what made Rayburn, Rayburn.

For decades, the Kirklands were highly respected in their industry and had a reputation for unquestionable standards of quality. In those early decades, they took turns filling every role in the company, from reading meters to paying bills to staying abreast of new advancements and regulations. Shannon Beber was hired as a temporary accountant in 2003 and ended up staying on full-time. Nothing was automated back then, so she managed all the accounts and financials manually. Most days, she unlocked the doors in the morning, worked all day, and locked the doors behind her as she left without ever seeing another person. For years.

She said, "I'm self-motivating, so it didn't bother me. There were only five of us, so somebody had to stay in the office and answer the phone. We all had to divide and conquer. To be honest, nobody had time to show me anything back then, so I didn't really know much about the field or the lines or the stations. There was an old map on the wall, so I knew what our territory kind of was, but I never went to a substation or anything."

Eddy Reece, the original transmission engineer decided in 2013 that it was time for Shannon to understand what kind of company she worked for after ten years of essentially working in isolation. He took her to see projects in the field to gain a better appreciation for what she was seeing on paper every day. As the accounts grew, Shannon's skills and expertise continued to evolve, and eventually, she moved out of accounting to become a project coordinator and is now the head of Project Coordination.

Shannon Beber's story is not uncommon. She is just one example of how Rayburn staff members have always taken advantage of opportunities to get educated beyond the jobs they were hired to do. This falls in line with the company's willingness to consider new and better ways to do things, even if it means shuffling people around or even risking losing them to other organizations because they become so valuable. It starts with being willing to question everything—in a healthy way.

A NEW POLICY

The Dallas metroplex exploded in every direction during the 1980s and 1990s. As demand grew, so did Rayburn. They couldn't continue to efficiently serve the needs of their Members with only five people, so the Kirklands continued slowly expanding. They doubled their workforce, adding David Naylor, who had previously consulted with them, along with many other highly experienced individuals. The balance sheet was relatively flat, but then in 2010, they acquired 25 percent of the Freestone Energy Center, for the first time moving from a transmission-only operation into power generation. This meant that they were able to produce some of the power themselves that they were selling to their Members, making them less dependent on other generators to meet loads.

In 2011, the company went from a balance sheet of less than a hundred million to $350 million due to acquisition and growth. They needed to bring in a CFO, so they began interviewing qualified candidates. One of these was David Braun. During his interview, he was given the balance sheet, and he said, "Oh, so this isn't just some sleepy little co-op?" (He is still being teased about that today.)

No, indeed. Rayburn was solidly out of the realm of sleepy co-op and into the big leagues. This was just the beginning of massive changes that the company was heading for.

There is a concept called the Satir Change Model that describes the process of how individuals experience and cope with change. The model is often used in organizational development to help individuals and groups cope with and adapt to change more effectively. It has five stages:

1. Late Status Quo: Familiar and comfortable, with possible underlying issues that need addressing.
2. Resistance: Introduction of a foreign element (a change or challenge) and subsequent resistance (fear, denial, etc.) to the change.
3. Chaos: Confusion, uncertainty, and vulnerability leading to opportunity for growth and learning.
4. Integration: Making sense of the change, learning new skills, and integrating new insights and understandings.
5. New Status Quo: New state of equilibrium, having adapted to the change.

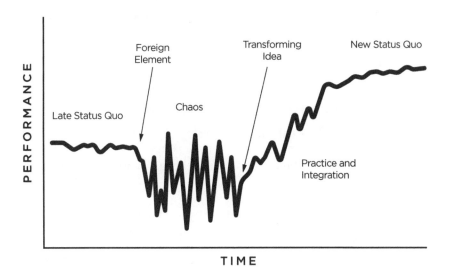

According to the Satir Change Model, things will continue as normal in any situation until a catalyst for change happens to challenge the old status quo. If a transforming idea emerges and is integrated and practiced, it can ultimately bring a new, healthier status quo moving forward.

Rayburn took the stance that they could either wait for that catalyst to come or they could be the catalyst themselves and force change upon themselves. Again, this attitude is hugely unusual in the electricity industry where safety and dependability are imperative.

Five years later, another particularly eye-opening disruptor served as a catalyst for change in October 2015. Board Member Mark Stubbs was there at the time. He said,

> Rayburn leadership was attending the annual meeting of one of their Members when a tornado ripped through the southern part of our territory. John Kirkland and David Naylor had to leave the meeting, get in their truck, and ride down to open switches. It just didn't dawn on

> me that this was still the case with Rayburn. Nothing
> was automated there yet. Here the President/CEO and
> Executive VP are getting in the truck and having to drive
> down to open a breaker to operate one of the substations.
> I couldn't believe it. That was the first time we started
> asking, "Does this make sense?"

This was when Rayburn officially began working to be more proactive rather than reactive.

The company finally hit the maturity level to face its first executive turnover in 2017. After thirty-two years, John and Annette Kirkland decided to hand over the reins. Eddy Reece followed shortly after. Fresh, new CEO David Naylor came to work on July 3, having just watched over eighty years' worth of combined experience walk out the door for the final time. This type of event can be catastrophic to organizations that are not equipped to embrace change.

David Naylor is quick to point out that there are internal disruptions and there are external disruptions that every organization faces at some point. Losing those three key, long-term experts provided a unique opportunity to be strategic and thoughtful in how Rayburn filled the gaps they left behind. He said:

> If there was one advantage to losing that much experi-
> ence, it was that nobody else knew what we did. We had
> to take a hard look at ourselves in the mirror and ask,
> "Does this all still make sense?" As we were bringing new
> people in, it became less about, "Let us tell you how we
> work and how things are done here." Instead, it was more
> like, "Don't worry about how we used to do things. We
> want you to look at what needs to get done and tell us
> how you want to accomplish that." It was a fresh look at

> everything we did as we added the expertise we needed. We weren't afraid to change the normal, day-to-day status quo of operating and challenge it to see if we needed to make things different or better for us.

Easy to say, but much harder to implement, particularly with a nonprofit that is overseen by a cooperative board of directors made up of the Members that Rayburn served. In a setup like this, there are many opinions and perspectives to consider before every decision. But that was not going to shackle the new Rayburn Co-op to archaic decision-making strategies or operational policies. In Naylor's 2017 State of the Cooperative presentation for the company, he laid out a new, official company policy: "Status Quo is Not Company Policy."

In that same address, Naylor said, "The enemy of excellence is complacency. I don't want people to just complain about problems. Come up with a solution. We have to embrace change to be successful. No one individual has the answers, so we need to create them together. So ask the hard questions and don't be afraid of the answer. Electricity is not a luxury. We don't mind spending money, but those consumers at the end of the line better be able to recognize the value we bring. If not, then we shouldn't be changing anything."

Rayburn's leadership maximized the opportunity of having new, fresh perspectives from the people that they were bringing in. Together, they examined every aspect of the company, from the smallest habits in day-to-day operations to chief policies and procedures.

Open and honest dialogue with all staff members became foundational to the Rayburn dynamic. As Board member John Ed Shinpaugh said, "Sacred cows make good steak."

The driving questions as they evaluated their company were:

1. What is it that we actually need to get done?
2. What's the very best way to do what needs to get done?

Further questions helped guide the decision-making process, including:

- Does this improve a process?
- Does it solve a problem?
- Is it consistent with our core values?
- Does it fit with our mission statement?
- Does it create value for our Members?
- Does it create benefits for our employees?
- Is it leading to fulfilling our vision?

When current COO Stephen Geiger came on board in 2017, he noticed the Rayburn difference right away.

> Where I came from, it was, "If it ain't broke, don't fix it." That mindset is very common in this industry. But at Rayburn, I was told that status quo was not company policy. That kind of mentality is shattering for this industry. It allows you to be nimble and flexible. It wasn't like, "Hey, do this because we've always done it this way." Instead, it was, "Does it work? Does it not work? No problem. Try something else." What we have been able to do in the six years since I came on board is nothing short of amazing.

As the company rapidly expanded, Rayburn was faced with increasingly bigger and more complicated decisions. The larger the company grew, the higher the stakes. Consultant Earl Shockley was also brought on board in 2017 because he offered more than **forty** years as a regulator in the industry. His germane observation **shows** the impact of this growth and the bravery that it took for **Rayburn** leaders to move into new realms:

> In a very short period of time, Rayburn has done what most people take ten or fifteen years to do. In the regulatory world, the power grid is regulated based on the activity you perform. Rayburn was originally in the distribution provider level, and they had maybe ten regulations that applied to them. When they got into the business of transmitting power, then their regulatory scrutiny went up to about eighty standards. The complexity got higher. Then it happened again when they moved into generation. That last move was a huge decision. It was going to take a lot of work. We've now put in place about 350 documents, including policies and procedures and auditable factors that make them compliant with the regulatory world. They are responsible for just about every rule under the code of federal regulations that apply to the power grid, including a large chunk of cybersecurity regulations.

Change can be intimidating, particularly when it brings **such** intense scrutiny. But courage provides the strength to try **anyway,** bounce back from mistakes, and build resilience. Jeff Lane has **been** on the Board of Directors for Rayburn since 2019. He said, "In **the** G&T world, it's, 'Do it the way we've always done it. Don't **question.'** But that's not the Rayburn way."

If your policy is to question everything and keep **improving,** courage has to come hand-in-hand. It is unsettling to break **away** from familiar patterns and routines, because of the risk of setbacks, failures, and disappointment. Stepping into the unknown and facing challenges is intimidating. The fear associated with risk keeps us from making decisions that may be difficult. Or, in some situations, we just don't want to get out of our comfort zone.

Lee Cockerell, former Executive Vice President of Operations for Disney World Resorts, tells a powerful story of the way he learned that improvement and change require effort. At the beginning of his career, he was the manager of a Marriott hotel in Philadelphia. He recalls the franchise owner Bill Marriott coming to visit him one day and requesting a tour of the hotel. As the two walked around and inspected the property, Marriot offered constant feedback to Cockerell. They eventually ended up behind the building in the loading and receiving dock where the dumpster was located. Because it was summer, there were a lot of flies, many of them making their way into the hotel and the onsite restaurants. When pressed on why he hadn't solved the problem, Cockerell tried to explain how challenging it was to get rid of the flies. Uninterested in the excuses, Marriott said:

> "Lee, if you have flies in your operation, it is because you like flies."

> I will never forget that moment and that lesson. What he meant, of course, is that you can get rid of those flies if you want to. You can order an enclosed dumpster. You can wash down the dumpster as many times a day as it takes so no flies will be there. You can install different insect control devices in that area. You can put fly fans on the loading dock doors, and on and on. Even if you have to buy one hundred fly swatters and issue them to

the employees with a quota each day, you can have an operation without flies.

So if you have rude employees, you must like that … If you have children with bad manners, you must like that. If you are not saving for your retirement, you must like that. If you don't exercise, you must like the way you feel and look … The problem with flies and other things we don't deal with is that they multiply. One fly today, ten flies tomorrow … One poor habit today, ten more next week.

You get rid of flies the same way you got them in the first place—one at a time.[3]

This may seem extremely harsh to some people, but the truth that Cockerell learned was that we have far more power over things than we often realize. If we claim to embrace change and improvement, we have to take responsibility for putting in the effort to drive that change and improvement. Just like the Rayburn leadership team did when eighty years' worth of experience retired, we have to be willing to identify and address issues, no matter how small they may seem. That is how we gain the power to create significant positive change.

---

3   Lee Cockerell, "Get rid of the flies," January 11, 2008, https://www.leecockerell.com/area-51-259/.

CHAPTER 3

BUILDING ON BEDROCK

My ultimate role is to protect the culture of Rayburn.

DAVID A. NAYLOR

Rub a balloon against your head, and what happens? Not only will your hair stand on end, but you can also have the delight of holding the balloon to the wall and leaving it to hang unaided.

What about scuffing your stocking feet along the carpet and touching another person? If you do it right, you'll both get a little shock. Even more fun if you do it in the dark.

In both of these common experiences, you are generating electricity through friction of two dissimilar materials. Most people call it static electricity, but the official name for it is "triboelectricity." This is the term used for the reaction that happens as electrons are transferred from one material to another. In other words, sparks fly when one gains electrons and the other loses them.

We see this same zero-sum principle in many other aspects of life, where one side wins and one side loses. Consider sports like tennis, where the total number of points remains the same. If one player wins a point, the other loses it. Success can only come when the other side fails. We see it when finite resources cannot match demand, such as the Tickle Me Elmo craze in 1996 or the great toilet paper shortage in the spring of 2020. When one person gets what they want, another person doesn't.

Traditional corporations promote zero-sum situations constantly. One position is filled out of many applicants. One person is promoted over others. Board voting power is designated in proportion to the number of shares owned. The majority shareholder is given the most weight when decisions are being made, meaning the bigger votes win, and everyone else loses.

This arrangement isn't the case with cooperative organizations like Rayburn. Every member gets an equal say, regardless of investment or seniority. One member, one vote. This egalitarian structure promotes a sense of fairness and community.

STAY TRUE TO THE FOUNDATION

As communications manager Gentry Ewing, says, "It's an exciting time to be in the utilities industry." The emotional and mental high that comes when we discover a new and better way to do something can be intoxicating, compelling us to seek out more "new and better" ways.

The shiny new object syndrome refers to the tendency of some leaders to frequently embrace new ideas, technologies, or management approaches without thoroughly considering their long-term implications. While innovation and adaptability are crucial for organizations to remain competitive, change for the sake of change can be counterproductive. Wise leaders avoid the urge to undergo frequent reorganization without a clear strategic purpose or thoughtful consideration of the impact on employees and productivity. Lack of stability erodes morale and fosters resentment, leading people to disengage and grow resistant. Routine upheaval made in the name of change leads to a lack of focus that often brings an apathetic or even negative atmosphere that drives away talented people who want a clear and defined role within an organized hierarchy. This doesn't begin to touch on the financial costs associated with any organizational adjustment.

To avoid these pitfalls, leaders are better off approaching organizational change with a strategic mindset, clearly communicating the reasons behind the changes and involving employees in the process. By fostering a culture of stability, transparency, and employee engagement, organizations can navigate necessary changes more effectively while minimizing the negative impacts.

The solution is to maintain a set of core values that cannot be questioned. In the corporate world, the term "core values" is used so often that it has almost lost meaning, but they are vital to the health and success of any organization. Call them foundational principles, organizational guidelines, underlying beliefs, or whatever you want. They are the fundamental elements of the way you do business—the traits that guide behavior and decisions within the entire organization. Core values serve as a moral compass, shape culture, and guide the overall direction of a company.

A defined set of values creates a shared identity and a common purpose, which helps build a cohesive and positive organizational culture. Choices that align with the values of the company enhance credibility both within and without the organization. This is richly evident within the Rayburn team. Values are the key element of the Rayburn decision-making framework.

As mentioned earlier, the four official Rayburn core values are: Integrity, Respect, Excellence, and Innovation. Rayburn believes these values are essential to success. Everything else can fall into place behind them. These four principles are the heart of the organization, the Rayburn DNA. If anything is non-negotiable, it is these traits.

INTEGRITY

- Integrity guides our business practices.
- We believe in transparency and honesty.
- We are committed to maintaining the highest standards of ethical conduct.
- We hold ourselves accountable to our Members, our employees, and our community.
- We are dedicated to operating with integrity in all of our interactions.

RESPECT

- Respect is deeply embedded in our company culture.
- We value diversity and inclusivity.
- We are committed to treating everyone with fairness, dignity, and respect.
- We believe that by fostering a culture of respect, we can build stronger relationships with our Members, our employees, and our community.

EXCELLENCE

- Excellence drives our company.
- We are committed to providing our Members with reliable and affordable energy.
- We are always striving to improve our services and operations.
- We hold ourselves to the highest standards of quality and efficiency, and we are dedicated to delivering the best possible service to our Members.

INNOVATION

- Innovation is the final pillar of our core values.
- We believe in challenging the status quo.
- We encourage our employees to think creatively and outside the box.
- We are committed to investing in innovation to better serve our Members and our community.

As Board member John Ed Shinpaugh said, "You can't just sit and watch your business. You have to live it and breathe it and be part of it. And you have to become a student of your industry. Rayburn has a tenacious appetite to leave no stone unturned and to use what they find, as long as it's best for the Rayburn employees or the four cooperative Members and our individual consumers. You can't take a middle-of-the-road position. The only thing I ever saw in the middle of the road was a dead skunk."

RAYBURN DNA

As a not-for-profit co-op, Rayburn benefits from being mission-driven in every aspect of the company. Of course, revenue matters, but Rayburn's leadership has the fortune of being able to focus on the main purpose of the company as much (or even more than) the bottom line. Their official mission is to "maximize the value of our Members' investment while maintaining competitive wholesale power costs as we exemplify integrity and excellence." In other words, Rayburn staff members are not constrained by a zero-sum game.

What makes this unusual is that they could very easily take their hands off the wheel and coast, knowing that at this point in the company's maturity, the electric power will get where it needs to go because the processes have long been put in place for things to run relatively smoothly. The company could coast, and nobody would blame them. That's the simplest way to run an electricity company. It is probably the more appealing approach too, because, as mentioned earlier, why question what works? You don't need to fix what ain't broken.

But this is not an organization that coasts. The freedom from zero-sum pressures has given rise to a culture at Rayburn like none other in this industry. The core values of Integrity, Respect, Excellence, and Innovation are emphasized to new employees from day one as the bedrock of Rayburn. It doesn't matter that nobody is forcing them to live these values because there is an internally generated desire to live up to them. In every department, people challenge themselves to add more value, find innovative strategies, and improve efficiencies.

Engineering Manager Scott Donham said, "Even though we are relatively small, our culture is strong. We are built around the bigger picture of what we're doing. We are providing a huge service to the community. We are keeping the lights on. That's what we're doing every day, and we want to find ways to do it better. Everybody here comes in with the same mentality. We know this from the day we are hired."

The dynamic in this company starts with that all-important openness to new ideas and willingness to change. This means people are flexible; whether being asked to refine a process, to solve a new problem, or even move to a different team, Rayburn people do it if that is best for the company. And they usually do it with a smile.

As a reward, Rayburn has very few restrictions when it comes to innovation, so staff members can push the limits of their imagination in terms of their jobs. The lines of what is acceptable are drawn along the values, but otherwise, there is no limit.

When Rayburn's people brainstorm new ideas, they know that some will stick and others won't, but that's all part of the process. As long as the mission and values are at the center, the conversations are easy. They start with the reason the company exists in the first place— to serve their Members. The troops are organized around that goal.

Rather than being project-focused, they are value-focused. This is unlike other organizations that often begin meetings with a discussion of deadlines or budgets or any other factor that could detract from what matters most. David Braun told a story about how this company culture guided them during a time of massive change. He said:

> Before David Naylor and I started working at Rayburn, the company was literally a paper G&T. This means

that all the company did was contract for power on a wholesale basis and resell it. Back then, Rayburn didn't even have their own meters or lines or anything.

At the time, the Board of Directors and John Kirkland determined that Rayburn would be able to serve their Members much better if they had their own meters instead of relying on someone else. The electric delivery company that owned everything at the time said, "Yep, you can change our meters for your meters. You've got twelve months. Go."

And so they had to hurry and go buy a bunch of meters, hook them all up, connect the communication so that they could read the meters, and everything else associated with that. They were literally working twelve- and fourteen-hour days, Saturdays, Sundays, and holidays. It didn't matter. They had until December 31, and they got the last of their meters hooked up on the 29th or 30th of December.

It would've been a whole lot easier to go, "You know what, we'll just keep using their meters because we don't think we can do this in twelve months."

That would've been the easy way out. But it always comes back to what's better for our Members. And if it means sacrificing a year of weekends and holidays, then that's what we're going to do.

This massive undertaking was similar to events that every new company has to face as it grows. When change happens quickly, particularly when it's something that hasn't been done before, you don't have time to overthink. You have to be able to trust that you have the right elements in place to make wise decisions and the right people ready to follow through with those decisions.

This is why culture is so crucial. David Naylor reflected on that time. "With all of those changes," he said, "I wanted to ensure we had the right mindset. Things were going so fast, and we could not look back. The company was not going to look the same tomorrow as it did yesterday, so we could either get overwhelmed, or we could embrace the challenge. It was a tremendous opportunity. But we couldn't look back and see what we did before because that memory didn't exist. In circumstances like that, you're creating the solutions by focusing on what makes sense for your mission. It's kind of like a boxing match in some ways. You're dodging and ducking the jabs right when they come."

LEADING EDGE NOT BLEEDING EDGE

Rayburn makes no secret that they are working toward being the best G&T in the nation. This means that the four core values are not empty rhetoric. Rayburn's people earnestly work on every single one of them every single day.

Innovation is at the core of every decision, driven by that firm belief that status quo should only be followed if it is truly in the best interest of the company and its Members. The phrase "push your comfort zone" is so ubiquitous, it's cliché. It's found in nearly every leadership, business, and self-help book. But clichés are clichés for a reason—they tap into some universal truth. Everyone knows doing the exact same thing day in and day out never leads to change. Lifting the exact same weight or running the exact same mileage will not bring greater strength, they just lead to maintaining the strength and speed from the previous day.

If innovation is one of your core values, you have to keep the right mindset or you risk losing focus and getting off course. For Rayburn, this means remembering that electricity is not a luxury. Many of the staff members use a mental picture to keep this as a focus: somewhere at the end of the line is a little widow, living on a fixed income, doing her best to pay the bills, and having barely enough money at the end of the month to make cookies for her grandkids.

This helps resist the temptation to think about the profit margins and the balance sheets first. The priority is making sure the rates that that sweet grandmother has to pay every month are fair for the electricity she is using.

But for corporations with millions of dollars at stake, it can be a little nerve-racking to use cost as the main focus instead of profit. When a fear of loss creeps in, we tend to back away from new opportunities and ignore the possibilities that might be available. Again, it's easy to do what you have always done.

With a strong, fundamental understanding of your mission and core values, it's possible to become comfortable investigating the edge of possibility. The term "cutting edge" is commonly used in technology, research, design, and even medicine. It metaphorically describes the forefront or leading position in a particular field, and the latest, most advanced developments. Being on the cutting edge implies that you have a commitment to staying ahead of the curve and are continuously pushing boundaries, giving you an advantage over others in your industry.

The phrase is obviously associated with the sharp edges of a knife, where the danger is. Instead of using the phrase "cutting edge," Rayburn leadership often uses the term "leading edge" instead. This implies you are balancing innovation with risk tolerance and preparation with innovation. To be leading edge, you must have a keen awareness of your resources as an organization, including your strengths and your weaknesses, to keep from getting too close to the bleeding edge. David Naylor elaborated:

> Despite the fact that innovation is one of our core values, we have to make sure it makes sense. Does it fit within the context of our company and our mission? We've seen a lot of innovation over the years, from improved processes to distributed resources to the purchase of a new power plant, and those all fit with what we needed to do. But if someone came in and said, "I think we should get into the airline industry," well that may be a great idea, but not for Rayburn. At least not today. We're not going to bounce from idea to idea without direction. We're going to make sure we do everything with excellence, and sometimes in order for people to be innovative, you have to have somebody who can handle those tasks that have to be done. You can make an argument that payroll is one of those tasks, right? There are certain things you have to do within payroll because nobody's working for free. It has to get done.

There is a principle called "The Goldilocks Effect" that explains how teams learn and grow best. Optimal growth happens when the challenge is not too small or too great, but just right. For companies that are growing quickly like Rayburn, challenges are best if they are just at the very edge of current abilities. Within fingertip's reach. When challenges are within fingertip's reach, they encourage teams to stretch, learn, and develop new skills without becoming overwhelmed or discouraged. This delicate balance between challenge and ability is the sweet spot where teams can experience the satisfaction of overcoming obstacles, building confidence, and continuously improving their performance.

PROACTIVE NOT REACTIVE

Knowing that proactive approaches are better than reactive approaches is common sense. A proactive approach gives organizations and individuals the security of knowing they are prepared in the event of unexpected events. It also provides optimal conditions for the achievement of goals and the discovery of new strengths and assets, leading to sustained success and resilience.

But knowing this concept is a lot different from actually practicing it. For most of those first decades while Rayburn was still a young company, it had no choice but to be reactive rather than proactive. It did not have the corporate maturity or resources to prepare for the future as much as the Board and the Executive Team wanted. The core employees spent their time in the essential, day-to-day tasks, troubleshooting problems if they came up through the use of contracted expertise and third-party providers.

In 2017, this mindset changed dramatically. Roles changed and responsibilities increased, and it now made sense to look more intently ahead for ways to develop and prepare for the future with a growing and developing workforce. Past mistakes proved instructive, and the Rayburn team was able to take the space and time to learn from them and plan ahead. As the years passed and the company continued to thrive, new staff members were added. Growth provided opportunities for employees to learn and be proactive in new ways.

Finding this space to learn has now become a standard practice. For example, HR makes a point to reach out to every new employee after three or four weeks to see how things are going. HR manager

Staci Bratcher said, "We ask them what they like and what they don't like. What are things we did well in the onboarding process and what could we have done better? This sets the tone that we are looking for honest feedback. They are always so blown away. I hear them say, 'HR wants to hear from me? That has never happened to me before. I have never had HR care for me as an individual.' This is what fosters the sense of community here, and what makes this such a great place to work. Rayburn has set a high bar in terms of culture. New employees always tell us that coming here is life-changing."

The running theme that HR and leadership hear from new hires is that they wish they had found Rayburn sooner.

TRUST BANK

In the long-term bestseller, *The 7 Habits of Highly Effective People* Stephen R. Covey introduced the metaphor "emotional bank account" as a description of the way trust works in relationships. If you think of a bank, we deposit money into our account to build up savings and we take it out when we need it. In an emotional bank account, we don't make the deposits, other people do. They make deposits of goodwill into our personal trust bank. These emotional deposits can include kindness, understanding, support, and effective communication.

In contrast, sometimes, we have to withdraw from someone else's trust bank by making a large request, offering constructive criticism, or admitting our mistakes and failures. Trust is also depleted through betrayal, harsh words, or dishonesty. There are times we know we are making a withdrawal from the goodwill we've instilled in someone else, such as when we ask for a big favor or when we need to share something that is hard to hear. In our strongest relationships, we work very hard to avoid the inadvertent withdrawals that come through arguments and disloyalty.

Covey suggests that maintaining a positive balance in each other's emotional bank accounts is crucial for healthy and successful relationships. When challenges or conflicts arise, having a surplus of positive emotional deposits can help buffer the impact of negative experiences. In a corporate setting, leaders set the tone for the importance of building and maintaining strong, positive connections with team members.

When done well, innovation and excellence can be big asks because both of these values push people to get uncomfortable. But people don't mind being challenged when there is plenty of trust in their emotional account.

Rayburn actively seeks out people who intrinsically understand the way the trust bank works, and who value relationships based on both honesty and respect. General Counsel Chris Anderson said:

> The attraction for me was the fact that I saw Rayburn as a tight-knit group of people who passionately cared about what they were doing. You can tell a culture fit almost right away by the way people operate and interact with each other. When I got here, it was above what I had previously experienced in my career, so I knew that it was different. The Executive Team told me they wanted someone to be a straight shooter with them. Not a yes man. In-house lawyers like me are beholden to our bosses. We have to keep them happy and make them look good. But we also have to protect them. It is our job to be the conscience of the company, that voice that speaks up if something is not going well. I have to be able to say what they might not want to hear. Here at Rayburn, they

are always willing to take all advice into account before making a decision. They trust me, and I trust them.

This kind of trust is built up over consistent deposits into the trust bank, and a willingness to admit when a withdrawal has been made—intentionally or not. In one instance, there was a fairly significant problem that began to affect the entire company. Once the Executive Team discovered the source of the problem, they were faced with the same decisions that leaders have when dealing with organizational issues. They could: (1) ignore it, (2) handle it quietly and hope nobody noticed how bad things had become, or (3) they could own it publicly and try to learn from the situation.

Rayburn's leadership chose the most challenging option—to get up in front of the entire company to acknowledge the situation and explain what happened. David Naylor took it upon himself to stand alone in front of all his employees and admit they had made a mistake and apologized to everyone for the negative fallout that had resulted. He explained how that mistake was being handled and what he hoped to see moving forward. He asked for forgiveness from those who had lost trust.

Accountant Erica Hilton voiced what most Rayburn employees felt at that moment. She said, "When the Executive Team acknowledged that failure, it was the beginning of re-establishing trust with everyone. Their transparency and genuine character started filling up the trust bank. I had never in my life seen an executive say, 'We failed' before. It blew my mind."

Since emotional bank accounts represent the balance of positive and negative emotional experiences and interactions, this meeting was a crucial step in recovering the company culture. The foundation had to be repaired so that those trust accounts could begin to be nourished back to a positive balance. Unsurprisingly, the company moved on quickly from this destabilizing event, and what had been a dark moment for the company became a positive pivot point based on how the situation was handled. When individuals have a history of positive interactions, they are more likely to give each other the benefit of the doubt and work toward resolution rather than escalating issues. The reservoir of positive feelings was deep enough to support the team through this challenge, and it became a valuable learning opportunity instead of a debilitating crisis.

OPEN-DOOR POLICY

In some companies, the Executive Team's involvement with staff might be restricted to a photo on the wall and an annual address. Most staff members in mid- to large companies probably know the names of the executives and possibly where their offices are located, but God forbid they should ever approach one of this elite cadre! If you have a problem or idea, take it up with your manager. You might even get to talk to your manager's supervisor if you're lucky. But beyond that, stay in your lane.

Not Rayburn. The open-door policy is as much a part of the company culture as the trust bank. There is never a break in the demand for electric power, so the Rayburn campus is full of activity around the clock, every day of the year. People are constantly moving from one place to another, coming and going, popping in and out of each other's offices. In fact, an argument could be made that the open-door policy is the way the trust bank is established.

The open-door policy works both ways. Managers and executives circulate throughout the departments regularly, and employees are encouraged to make connections with others in and out of their departments. The message is repeated at every meeting, "Rayburn really does have an open-door policy." Some people eagerly take advantage of it. Others don't.

As Gentry Ewing said, "Some people prefer their independence and like to stay focused on their day-to-day tasks. They are naturally introverted." In other cases, people might be afraid to talk to a CEO based on prior experiences in other companies. But David Naylor has made it his mission to make sure the open-door policy is fully implemented and internalized by every single employee, and he does this by exemplifying it personally. He knows some people might feel less comfortable coming to visit him in his office, so he takes the "open door" to them to provide an opportunity for conversation.

He is highly visible in the company every day, stopping now and then to have an informal chat. He intentionally doesn't ask questions that might feel like he's checking up on people but rather invites them to share what is going on in their lives and what is important to them. What happened this weekend? How are your kids? Did your team do well in the game?

Ask enough goodwill questions like this, and any nervousness that might have existed dissolves during those brief conversations. The hope is that when a real problem comes up, they will feel safe and comfortable enough to approach him or any other manager because the trust bank is full.

All of the managers are encouraged to follow his example. CIO Chase Snuffer is the manager of the IT department. He said, "I am not naturally like that, to go out of my way to talk to people. We in IT are very much reserved in that regard, to the extreme of shyness sometimes. But now I make sure to come out of my office to let everyone know my door is open. That's how you maintain the trust bank, and then whenever you have to make a withdrawal for whatever reason, you have some currency there. I have seen how it works. People in IT are coming out of their shells now."

It is human nature to want to speculate and process when things are not going according to expectations. This is how misunderstandings are made and rumors begin to spread, the quickest way to destroy company culture. When David stood before the company and talked about that mistake, he made sure to remind everyone that the open-door policy was very much in effect. He encouraged anyone who had questions, concerns, or lingering doubts to come directly in and talk to him or anyone else on the Executive Team.

The open-door policy goes above the Executive Team as well. David makes a point to have one-on-one conversations with every Board member at least once a quarter, if not more. The trust bank is crucial with these Members because they are ultimately the keepers of Rayburn's fate. If they lose trust in David and the Executive Team, they are obliged to make changes for the good of the company. Consequently, the leadership at Rayburn wants to keep their trust bank full with the Board as well. They need to know that Board decisions are based on the same desire for the good of the consumers at the end of the line.

Open doors are best when they swing two ways.

FLAT ORGANIZATION

Why did the manager bring a map to work every day? To find his way through the chain of command!

OK, terrible joke, but you get the point. It may not be very funny, but in many large organizations, it kind of hits home. There are layers of authority in a typical organizational chart, with each person reporting up the line until you get to the tip of the triangle with the CEO or president.

Hierarchies like this can take on a militaristic view. Have you ever watched an old war movie where the commander barks an order to his men? Then, a random subordinate repeats that order, and another one does the same thing, and then again down the line until the soldier at the bottom performs the order. They all wait until the commander gives another order. Nobody moves without the say-so of the person above them.

This mimics the experience many people have when working in large corporations. Engineer Manager Scott Donham worked for a defense contractor before coming to Rayburn, and his experience there was typical of this strictly organized structure. He said:

> I had a supervisor and then a manager and then a deputy director and then a director over my department. Let's say I needed something, maybe a software fix. If I went to my counterpart on the software side directly to ask for it, he'd say, "I can't. I have to get that task assigned from my manager."
>
> So, I'd have to go to my supervisor, who would go to the manager, who would then have a manager meeting with the other department. It was my supervisor to my manager to their manager to their supervisor to that person. And then back. That was the quickest path to get things done—five layers away. That's if it all worked well. If they disagreed, they'd have to go to the deputy directors to see what they thought, and then it would come back down. It could take weeks of wasted hours of

bureaucracy for something as simple as a thirty-minute software problem.

A flat organization, on the other hand, is a type of organizational structure that has few or no levels of middle management between the staff and the executives. In a flat organization, there are typically only a few layers of hierarchy, and employees often have a broader scope of responsibilities and more autonomy compared to traditional hierarchical structures.

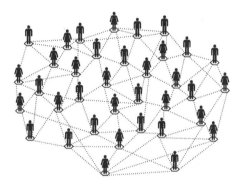

This is what Rayburn espouses. Instead of a traditional pyramid structure with many levels of management, there may be only a few or even just one. Decision-making authority is often pushed down to lower levels in the organization, which allows for quicker decision-making and more autonomy for employees. Because of this, individual employees are generally more flexible and adaptable to change. With fewer layers of bureaucracy, information can flow quickly, and the entire organization can respond more rapidly to challenges and opportunities.

COO Stephen Geiger said, "Here, there is no chain of command, per se. Don't get me wrong though. At the end of the day, David Naylor is ultimately on the line because he's answerable to the Board.

But anyone can go directly to him with questions, suggestions, and problems. They don't have to get permission from their manager first. It's not like you have to come to me, get my blessing, and then go talk to him. There are no barriers like that."

This can be a bit of a culture shock to new hires. Linemen who come from other companies, for example, constantly express delight at the way their requests are handled. The standard process in other places too often follows the old hierarchy, where they have to request things formally and wait sometimes months while that request goes through three or four levels of management before they get what they need. If they are lucky.

Recently, some of Rayburn's linemen had realized they needed a particular piece of equipment to be more efficient and effective, a side-by-side offroad vehicle that would allow them to travel over nearly any type of terrain. David Braun said, "We had just been discussing the best way to get them what they needed when one of the guys happened to drive by a dealer and saw that two of them were on sale. They were last year's models, but they were still brand new. He called me and told me about the sale. I told him to just go get them. He didn't have to wait for a complicated request for capital and all that. We had already discussed it. We knew they needed them, so why wait?"

This is a wonderful model for efficient and effective communication, but it does come with some challenges. When HR requested David Naylor create an org chart to give to new hires, they weren't especially happy with what he gave them. As you can imagine, it wasn't the upside-down, tree-like shape that we are all familiar with. Instead, it was a chaotic cluster of titles clumped here and there, color-coded based on what room they worked in. His name wasn't even on it. True to the culture, HR had to laugh and let go of the idea that this type of unique structure was going to be neatly defined on paper. Open communication in a flat organization is kind of a messy thing, but it works wonders. It allows an organization to be agile, efficient, and to have the ability to adapt to change, both known and unknown.

HANDS-OFF LEADERSHIP

Another crucial element of the trust bank is giving people the space to do their jobs. Nobody likes to have a supervisor looking over their shoulder all the time. This management style often has the opposite effect from what they want. Micromanagement negatively impacts both individuals and the overall work environment. Common effects include: less trust, impaired team collaboration, decreased morale, reduced job satisfaction, increased stress and burnout, high (and costly) turnover rates, decreased productivity, wasted time, and stifled creativity and innovation.

Micromanagement erodes trust as it conveys a lack of confidence in the abilities and judgment of team members. When employees feel that their every move is being scrutinized and that their manager lacks trust in their abilities, it can create a negative and demoralizing work atmosphere. Instead of working cohesively, team members may become focused on pleasing the manager individually, leading to a breakdown in teamwork and collaboration. They may feel frustrated and unfulfilled when they are not given the autonomy and freedom to perform their tasks in a way that aligns with their skills and expertise. The ability to think critically and creatively is hampered as the pressure to meet detailed, scrutinized expectations leads to fear of making mistakes. Often employees in these conditions grow so dissatisfied that they choose to leave, taking institutional knowledge with them and requiring an investment to retrain and re-educate their replacement.

To create a healthier work environment, managers need to find a balance between providing guidance and allowing employees the autonomy to excel in their roles. Rayburn leadership recognizes the importance of keeping their hands off the wheel as much as possible. If an employee has been given a responsibility, they are allowed to do what they need to do to succeed. This kind of trust is critical. It is built one small step at a time, trusting as you hand over more and more responsibility. With each success, a higher level of trust is earned. Scott Donham shared what it was like to be a technical engineer at Rayburn before moving into the Manager role. He said:

> I feel like that's been a big factor in what's made Rayburn, Rayburn. The trust that we had in John Kirkland, and now the trust that we have in David Naylor. It's what makes Rayburn really nimble. The culture that we built here lets us progress and do things a lot quicker than you would expect from a company of this size. I was always given the ability to try new things. If I wanted to test a new product, for example, I was told, "Go ahead and buy one and try it out. If it works, we'll put it in every station." I have always felt supported when trying to innovate, and now I'm able to turn around and give the same thing to my team.

When each person is trusted to make smart decisions, the entire organization becomes a living, breathing organism of its own. As long as people get their jobs done and keep their managers informed, the company is allowed to run the way it needs to run. This type of culture is irreplaceable during a crisis. When four tornadoes hit the Rayburn service area in 2017, it was all-hands-on-deck. Three tornadoes directly hit Rayburn transmission lines, wiping out the power supply. Within forty-eight hours, everything was restored because people knew their jobs, they were trusted to do those jobs well, and they had long established the open communication needed to reach out when they needed support. Effective leadership is a balance between empowering and trusting team members while still providing guidance and support.

MISTAKES ARE OK

The fear of failure is a powerful force that can erode the trust bank faster than just about anything else. Nobody wants to believe they are a micromanager, but there are traits to watch for that might indicate you may need to rethink your approach. If you feel a strong need to control the outcome of projects, have a perfectionist mindset, or resist delegating out of fear of mistakes, that is often a sign that your relationships are not built on trust. These habits will be interpreted as a lack of confidence in your team's abilities.

To combat this, leaders have to accept that mistakes are going to happen and believe in their team enough to know that they can be handled. Failure avoidance is not a productive mindset if you believe in pushing the status quo. It's scary enough to be on the leading edge, but if you add the pressure to be perfect, you will destroy all confidence and you will either shrink back from the front or you will fall off the edge entirely.

Risk tolerance means mistake tolerance. Stephen Geiger said:

> We all know that Rayburn leadership has our backs 100 percent. And we have theirs. That's the trust that we all have. This gives you the flexibility to try new things based

> on good data and reasonable ideas. We're not going to
> just flippantly decide things because we don't want to
> disappoint them. But even if we do, they will support us.
> We're incumbent to do our best to make good decisions,
> and if it ends up that we made the wrong one, we'll have
> a conversation about that. Everybody is empowered at all
> levels to make decisions. We're still accountable for them,
> but we are always free to try.

Tolerating mistakes in the workplace is important because it fosters a culture that embraces a healthy approach to innovation and creativity. Some people are more self-aware than others, and that can be a challenge. If someone can't be trusted to be smart, that's not good for anyone. When employees feel safe to make and admit mistakes, it creates a culture of continuous learning. Analyzing errors allows individuals and teams to understand what went wrong, why it happened, and how to improve processes moving forward. When that happens, they are more likely to take calculated risks and explore innovative ideas, knowing that the organization understands the inherent risks and supports a culture of experimentation. They are more likely to take ownership of their work and be actively involved in transparent communication and collaboration.

As an added bonus, leaders who tolerate mistakes are more likely to create an environment where their team members feel comfortable taking on new leadership roles. Rather than viewing mistakes as failures, they see opportunities for refinement and enhancement.

Another common, but less discussed effect comes from being afraid of making mistakes. Chase Snuffer explained:

> One of the things that I have experienced in the past at
> other companies is when a mistake occurs or something

happens, even if it is a small thing, it typically ends up creating red tape. We're going to create a small process or something, a checkpoint signature, something that's going to happen so that whatever it was doesn't happen again. I think that to some degree, that's fine to do, but I think for most mistakes, it should be a learning experience. A trainable moment to help us learn and get better.

What you see when red tape builds up over time is that your efficiencies go away. We're just going to add this one little thing. No big deal. Well, that's fine. Two weeks later, something else happens and now we're just going to add this other little thing. Those little things add up to where now this simple process takes a long time.

Having the latitude to make mistakes, to create teachable and coachable moments, and to have permission to move on from that point has been very refreshing here at Rayburn. We do a very good job of moving quickly on from things and being adaptive. And if you don't allow for those mistakes to happen, you become less maneuverable, and everything just slows to a crawl.

The freedom to make mistakes is another one of David Naylor's constant reminders in company meetings. He says, "We believe in you. We encourage you. We've all made plenty of mistakes, and that's to be expected. Don't be afraid. We're not perfect either. This is not about perfection. Mistakes are not cause for termination; they are cause for learning. We'll do what we need to do to move on."

That little autonomy is very empowering. People really start to fly when they feel trusted. Rayburn leaders know there are always two sides to every story and work hard to be sure they are asking the right questions when mistakes happen. Do employees not understand their role? Do they not understand what tasks to do? Is the best option to provide more training?

Mistakes don't have to be the end of the world. With a healthy sense of humor, they can even be a source of entertainment rather than shame. David Naylor proved this when one employee totaled his company truck. She was driving David's assigned company vehicle and pulled into traffic. Unfortunately, she did not notice an oncoming truck. It apparently did not notice her either because it hit her with full force, not even touching the brakes. After three full spins, she found herself in an adjacent parking lot, listening to OnStar asking if she needed an ambulance. Fortunately, she was OK, although she had to crawl across the seat to the passenger side to exit the truck.

As anyone would be, she was very worried that there would be harsh consequences for crashing her boss's vehicle. But upon hearing about the accident, the Executive Team was far less concerned about the truck than they were about her well-being. To her surprise, the consequences included an outpouring of support and care. And now, they all have one more funny story to add to the camaraderie of the company. David said, "It's not like you've made a mistake, so therefore you're out. That's not the way we work. This is not about perfection. That's where the trust element comes in here. We understand that mistakes are going to be made, so we'll do what we need to do. Let's all learn and move on."

CHAPTER 4

ABOVE AND THEN BEYOND

We want to hire smart people who can tell us what to do.

DAVID A. NAYLOR

Aristotle was attributed as saying, "The whole is greater than the sum of its parts." Most people don't realize that what he actually said was, "The whole is something besides the parts." Aristotle knew that the "whole" doesn't always end up being greater than the pieces that make it up. Sometimes, it is different. And sometimes, it is worse. Imagine the "parts" include a lit match, a piece of paper, and physical contact between the two. We end up with a pile of ashes. Hard to argue that the "whole" from the combination of those parts is greater than they were before they came together.

This concept applies to both physical and abstract systems, like groups of human beings. When individuals come together in a team, the resulting dynamic can lead to outcomes that are better, worse, or simply different from what each member could achieve alone. Researchers and leaders have long studied teamwork to try to understand how to bring the best out of each team member in a way that produces a new and better whole. By examining the factors that contribute to successful teamwork, such as communication, collaboration, and trust, effective leaders learn how to harness the unique strengths of each member and work toward a common purpose that exceeds what any single person could accomplish independently. To outperform the sum of their individual parts.

CHANGE IN THE WORKFORCE

A famous single-frame comic strip by Sidney Harris shows two scientists standing at a large blackboard, looking at each other. A formula is scribbled across the left side of the board. There is a gap in the middle of the board with only the words "Then a miracle occurs," followed by more complicated numbers and symbols. The caption below reads, "I think you should be more explicit here in step two."[4]

The "miracle" that Harris cleverly notes is a real phenomenon called "emergence." Researchers, philosophers, scientists, and even artists have long sought to grasp this mysterious ingredient that, if somehow properly defined, could explain the fascinating phenomena of change. Emergence is the word used to describe distinct outcomes, patterns, and behaviors that arise from the combination of separate elements in a complex system. It is that "something" that happens when the sum of parts becomes a new and different whole.

To take it further, emergence describes how the defining qualities of a system are not simply the sum of the properties of its individual parts but rather the qualities that emerge from the interactions and relationships among these parts. This concept is observed in various domains such as in the behavior of ant colonies, the transition of

---

4   "Science Cartoons Plus," accessed April 12, 2024, http://www.sciencecartoonsplus.com/index.php.

matter, and the emergence of life from simple elements. Managers, supervisors, executives, and researchers have long sought to understand how to encourage the emergence of a functional team in the workplace from the combination of independent human beings. But this understanding doesn't come easy, especially today.

The American workplace has undergone significant changes over the last century, influenced by various factors such as technological advancements, demographic shifts, economic changes, and societal trends. According to the Bureau of Labor Statistics, in the twentieth century, the American workforce increased roughly sixfold, from 24 million in 1900 to 139 million in 1999.[5] This growth was accompanied by changes in the composition, compensation, and nature of work. Through the decades, as manufacturing jobs declined, they were replaced with service-oriented and knowledge-intensive sectors. The workforce is more diverse in age, ethnicity, background, and gender, and organizations are finding new and innovative ways to adapt to these changes.

A report from the McKinsey Global Institute found that the COVID-19 pandemic had a new and significant impact on the workforce. In the years leading up to the pandemic, the U.S. workforce continued to grow, reaching 157.5 million in 2019.[6] The pandemic had a significant impact on the labor market, with 8.6 million occu-

5   Donald M. Fisk, "American labor in the 20th century," US Bureau of Labor Statistics, accessed April 12, 2024, https://www.bls.gov/opub/mlr/cwc/american-labor-in-the-20th-century.pdf.

6   "Civilian labor force by age, sex, race and ethnicity," US Bureau of Labor Statistics, accessed April 12, 2024, https://www.bls.gov/emp/tables/civilian-labor-force-summary.htm.

pational shifts taking place from 2019 through 2022.[7] This shift was far more drastic than the changes observed during a typical year, with lasting, and in some cases, permanent effects. Millions of people left their previous roles, with some finding more appealing jobs in a completely new occupation for any number of reasons, including higher pay, more flexibility, greater appreciation, better fit, or increased opportunities for growth. Career-long employment within the same company is a thing of the past.

Technology played a crucial role in shaping the American workplace before the pandemic, but it has become even more entrenched in the American workplace. The rapid advancement of digital technologies, automation, and artificial intelligence was already transforming the nature of work and the skills required to succeed in the modern economy. The pandemic accelerated this trend, forcing many organizations to adopt remote work arrangements and digital collaboration tools to maintain business continuity. The massive uptick in demand for remote work, combined with reduced availability of talent in specialized fields due to retirement and career switching has spurred a retention crisis in some industries.

Attracting and retaining talent has been a headline issue for organizations nationwide. A recent Forbes article titled "Beyond Money: The Real Reasons Employees Stay or Leave"[8] stated that less than 10 percent of employees who leave their jobs do it because of money. Most leave for more personal reasons around their ability or inability to fit into a company culture. And to make matters even more chal-

---

7   Kweilin Ellingrud, Saurabh Sanghvi, Gurneet Singh Dandona, Anu Madgavkar, Michael Chui, Olivia White, and Paige Hasebe, "Generative AI and the future of work in America," McKinsey Global Institute, July 26, 2023, https://www.mckinsey.com/mgi/our-research/generative-ai-and-the-future-of-work-in-america.

8   Shep Hyken, "Beyond money: the real reasons employees stay or leave," Forbes, July 9, 2023, https://www.forbes.com/sites/shephyken/2023/07/09/beyond-money-the-real-reasons-employees-stay-or-leave/?sh=5593e98e3d07.

lenging, the quiet-quitting trend that emerged post-pandemic was equally or possibly more detrimental to organizations than employee turnover.

A well-established company culture is one of the most crucial elements in combating the loss of staff. Healthy team dynamics remain a cornerstone of success in today's interconnected and fast-paced business world. While brilliant minds working in isolation can sometimes achieve great things, teams made up of people with diverse skill sets, experiences, and perspectives almost always outperform individuals over the long run.

While Rayburn provides for some flexibility for employees to work from home, it encourages, and frankly prefers, employees to work onsite. "Despite gains in technology, it's not uncommon to see employees grab a conference room and brainstorm on a whiteboard to solve a problem or overcome a challenge. That spontaneous collaboration and dynamic is fun to watch," says David Naylor.

TEAM EFFORT

Rayburn culture is not a hard sell when hiring. It is attractive to anyone who has worked in a more traditional, slower-moving, less courageous organization. Even though the company has been around for decades, it feels exciting, young, and fresh, the way a start-up does. This is a unique company in that regard. Its rich history is combined with an innovative spirit. General Counsel Chris Anderson said, "I'm not going to go backward. When I came here, I knew that it was different, so I was getting in on the ground floor of this growth. You don't have to retrofit or change people. It's more about how we all help take this flame and help fan it to grow."

Sara Richard was hired as a staff attorney very early in her career, confident she would catch the vision. She said, "At the Rayburn job interview, they were talking about the culture, and I was like, 'Oh my gosh, this place sounds amazing.' I didn't even know what a cooperative was before I came here, to be honest. I had only worked for one firm while I was in school, but the culture here and the people surprised me. Everyone really works together as a team to help each other."

This team environment is a huge factor in the success of Rayburn. We all know that organizations that prioritize and cultivate effective teamwork are better positioned to navigate challenges and achieve long-term success. When people work together well, they can often accomplish more than the sum of their individual efforts, leading to higher efficiency and productivity. Everyone contributes their unique expertise, leading to a more comprehensive and effective approach to solving complex problems. Likewise, as they learn from each other, share knowledge, and pass along new skills, they contribute to the overall growth of the company. Perhaps most importantly, high-functioning teams can adapt more quickly to changes and emergencies, providing an advantage over slower-moving competitors.

Accountant Erica Hilton said, "It's truly a team environment. I have never once heard anyone at Rayburn say, 'That's not my job.' That's huge. People here are genuine and authentic, and they clearly want to help each other. I had thirty years in corporate America before coming here, and so when I showed up at this place, I kept waiting for the other shoe to drop. Nobody is this good. But it's been over two years, and I'm starting to think there is no other shoe."

GROWTH BRINGS CHALLENGES

Growth is a double-edged sword. On the one hand, expansion is the result of—or reach for—more customers, revenue, and opportunities. But scaling up also brings the risk of straining the organization's resources to the breaking point if not done deliberately or thoughtfully. Speedily hiring and training large numbers of new people without losing the spark that makes your company special presents a real challenge. The logistics become complicated as well. Simple considerations can pile up: Do you have enough computers for all the new staff? Is your office space big enough? Can your inventory and equipment handle double the orders? Or will customers wind up frustrated by a lack of consistency and long waiting periods?

In the perilous journey of a company's growth, the risk of financial and organizational instability looms large, casting a shadow over even the most promising projects. As organizations navigate the treacherous waters of maturity, they often find themselves grappling with the ever-present threat of cash scarcity, a merciless adversary that can swiftly drain the lifeblood from even the most robust of enterprises. In the dance between expenditure and revenue, companies must delicately balance the weighty demands of salaries and inventory against the elusive promise of customer payments. Should this delicate equilibrium be disrupted, and the coffers run dry before profits are seen, the very growth that once seemed a beacon of hope can swiftly transform into a harbinger of doom.

The work itself gets more complicated as well. That happy little start-up that felt like a family becomes a web of departments, suppliers, and budgets that are tricky to manage. Lose focus in the churn, and quality as well as cohesiveness may start slipping through the cracks.

Big growth brings big rewards, but it carries big risks, too. Successful leaders have the foresight and wisdom needed to identify critical junctures while building from a firm foundation that can withstand the weight of growth without buckling under the strain. Do that, and the sky's the limit. Stumble, and you could be one of those promising start-ups that flames out because you grew too far, too fast.

This was most certainly a concern for Rayburn. Shannon Beber, who was hired in 2004 and has witnessed the company's transformation firsthand, said, "I was here essentially dormant for thirteen years, sitting alone, answering phones, and talking to myself. I loved my job, but nothing ever changed. Then it got really exciting. When you quadruple in size in just a few years like we did, things change so fast." As Rayburn grew, the close-knit family atmosphere that had been a hallmark of the company's early days faced the risk of unraveling. With its rapid expansion and influx of new employees, maintaining a sense of camaraderie and shared purpose became increasingly challenging. The once tight-knit group of five now found themselves surrounded by unfamiliar faces, and the fear of losing the company's unique culture loomed large.

The family feel of Rayburn has been a persistent source of pride and strength for the company and preserving it through periods of explosive growth has been a top priority. Shannon added, "I was fearful that we weren't going to be able to maintain the culture we had always had. With every step we took, there were growing pains." However, despite the challenges, Rayburn managed to stay true to its core values while embracing the dynamics of growth. Through open communication, employee engagement initiatives, and a conscious effort to foster a sense of belonging, the company has successfully navigated the delicate balance between expansion and preservation. "It's amazing to me how we have been so dynamic, but we have stayed the same too," Shannon added, reflecting on the company's ability to adapt without compromising its identity. As Rayburn continues to grow, the commitment to maintaining and strengthening the family-like culture remains unwavering, ensuring that the spirit of together-ness that has defined the company from the beginning will endure for years to come.

Rayburn Growth: Number of Employees

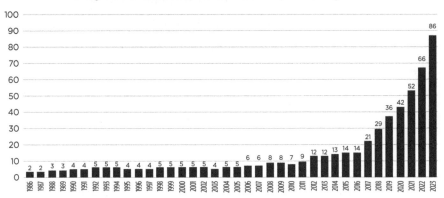

Rayburn Growth: Plant in Service ($Million)

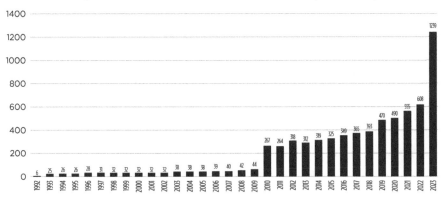

Scott Donham was full-time employee number fifteen when he started in 2015. He was actually the last person hired for attrition, which means the dozens of people hired since then were hired for growth. He came on board when Rayburn was still fairly quiet. He said, "We didn't do much compared to what we do today. It was more just sort of maintaining, making sure everything was working smoothly. We didn't ask questions like, 'What can be built?' or 'How can we grow?' It's definitely an interesting thing to be at a company that was so small, but then has grown so much. Seven years at most companies isn't a lot of time, but after eight years here I'm already one of the long-term employees."

Chase Snuffer has had a similar experience, having come on in 2017 as the singular IT guy. As of 2024, his department was twenty-five people and counting. This kind of lightning-fast growth might be expected and common in other industries that have a start-up company environment, but for utilities, it is unheard of.

Rayburn had no playbook of success or failures to follow from other companies that had done the same thing, which brought advantages and challenges. Most of the people came in with no preconceived ideas about the company culture because, as David Naylor pointed out, "Most of our employees had never even heard of a cooperative until they joined Rayburn." This is a huge advantage because nobody came in with ideas about what it should or shouldn't be. But at the same time, it was a challenge because they had to be trained about what was expected. As it grew, Rayburn continued to make a deliberate effort to hire with a purpose, always using culture as a compass.

As Chris Anderson said, "We didn't hire to make them co-op employees per se. We hired to meet our business needs and built a new form of G&T in the process—that is the secret sauce that begins to emerge here and really comes through later." This approach allowed Rayburn to cultivate a unique identity, one that blended the best of cooperative principles with the agility and innovation needed to thrive in an evolving industry. By staying true to its core values while embracing change, Rayburn has set itself apart as a trailblazer, forging a path that others may soon follow.

David Naylor calls the period of explosive growth the "awkward teenage years" of Rayburn because they are still working out how to define the Rayburn identity as it encompasses the addition of people of many different demographics. In the electric industry (particularly in cooperatives), companies tend to be filled with older men who have been working in the field their whole lives. As mentioned in chapter 1, they have often inherited the job from fathers and even grandfathers. Because of this, the hand down of knowledge and training happens without many formal procedures and processes. Factors like maintaining a company culture aren't usually one of the main concerns inside the walls of most electric co-ops throughout the United States.

But Rayburn isn't like most electric co-ops, so as it grew, leaders insisted on making culture a key element of the planning discussions. They persisted in working to figure out how to establish and maintain a strong company culture from scratch that held fast despite all the changes that were happening. This culture had to be true to the foundations of the company while still being attractive to all of its staff members, despite demographic differences. It had to work for all genders, ages, educational levels, backgrounds, job titles, etc. Most importantly, the culture had to embody the spirit of excellence, curiosity, and courage that were pillars of Rayburn from the very start. The approach to growth began and remains centered on culture, as created by David Naylor and his team. This is exhibited through who they have hired and how David and his Executive Team continue to address Rayburn's growth challenges.

IT STARTS WITH HIRING

Variations of the famous quote, "Surround yourself with people who are smarter than you," have been attributed to everyone from Steve Jobs to Stephen Covey. And for good reason. If you are a manager, leader, executive, or company owner, there are four key reasons why hiring people smarter than yourself is often considered a wise business strategy:

1. It pushes you to keep learning and staying sharp. Working with smart, talented people keeps you challenged. You can't rest on your laurels or get complacent, because your team members are raising the bar. Their example pushes you to continue developing your own skills and knowledge.

2. It brings fresh ideas, innovations, and solutions. Smart people think differently than you do. Those different perspectives spark creativity, debate, and innovation.

3. It propels the company forward faster. A team of sharp, talented people can simply accomplish more than an average team. There is momentum when you have a crew of smart, efficient team members rowing in sync. Difficult tasks seem more achievable, and roadblocks are more easily overcome.

4. It makes leadership easier. Smart people require less hand-holding to do their jobs well. They take initiative, anticipate issues, and solve many problems without needing approval or oversight. That frees up a manager's time to focus more strategically on big-picture items. With smart teams, an organization can hum along smoothly with less effort required to steer it.

The key is checking your ego at the door. Generally, surrounding yourself with sharp people pays off hugely if you can avoid becoming defensive or threatened. David Naylor said, "It's really just a matter of getting the right people. We want to hire smart people who can tell us what to do."

This approach requires a high level of self-awareness and humility from leaders, recognizing that the collective intelligence of a diverse and talented team far outweighs individual expertise. This is one instance when the whole can (and should) always be considered greater than the sum of the parts. By fostering an environment where ideas are valued based on their merit rather than the status of the person presenting them, Rayburn has been able to tap into the full potential of its workforce.

This mindset is clear during the hiring process, as it permeates every aspect of the company's culture. Before even being offered a position, open communication, active listening, and constructive feedback are demonstrated to potential new hires during the team interview process. This creates a space where the new employee comes on board feeling empowered on day one to share their insights and challenge the status quo. Rayburn leadership demonstrates their understanding that their role is not to have all the answers but to facilitate the discovery of the best solutions through collaboration and mutual respect.

Board member Jeff Lane said, "We all know our employees are our biggest asset, and the executives at Rayburn do well to recognize that. David Naylor and his team have the knack for bringing the right people in at the right time."

Attracting and retaining talent was always top of mind for the Rayburn Executive Team. But they are not satisfied to stop there. It's one thing to find and hire "A" talent and another entirely to keep them. Naylor said, "How do you lead a company that values both the high achievers and the worker bees? You have to value them the same, but you're also valuing them differently."

To lead a company that values both types of workers, it is important to recognize and appreciate the unique contributions of each group. High achievers often drive innovation and growth, while workers are essential for the smooth functioning of daily operations. Key strategies for achieving this include setting clear roles and responsibilities, fostering effective communication, a system of acknowledgment and rewards, and appropriate support and development.

The predominant sentiment among all staff members at Rayburn is a willingness to constantly question constructively, press ahead, and adapt without sacrificing a spirit of excellence. This has created an environment where anyone, no matter their role, can share innovative ideas and propose solutions and be acknowledged in their contributions. It is imperative to build a culture of gratitude, loyalty, and collaboration that encourages and recognizes the efforts of every employee. The key feature of this is how leaders provide support and opportunities for development. Staff members benefit from access to resources that further their innovative ideas, in conjunction with ongoing training and upskilling to enhance operational efficiency.

At Rayburn, this support starts at the very first interaction—the recruitment. The Rayburn hiring process is the first step in training staff members on the company culture. A top predictor of a new hire's success or failure is their attitude, making it a critical factor in the hiring process. James Wallace said, "When I first came here, the interview just blew me away. My first impressions of the company didn't even feel real. They took me on a tour of the place, and I was amazed at what I saw. It was all about cultural fit, and I was sold."

One of the greatest compliments an organization can receive is when staff members do the recruiting. When a person loves their job and feels that it is a positive place to be, they are more eager to share it with people they trust. That has certainly been the case at Rayburn. For example, every one of the linemen has worked with at least one other lineman before coming on. They consistently reach out to people they know who are top performers when openings occur. This indicates the level of trust they have in the company to want to bring their friends in. Today, a majority of new hires come highly recommended by current employees who are well respected and trusted. As Stephen Geiger said, "They're not going to stick their necks out for somebody who is just going to skate by. It's almost like a self-fulfilling prophecy. You make the environment such that people want to be here, and then, sure enough, they do."

That referral carries a lot of weight because, as James Wallace said, "Anybody can put on an act for forty-five minutes. You can't really know somebody in that amount of time. But if somebody else knows them, maybe knows their family, spent time with them outside of work, and knows their habits and their personality, that speaks volumes. Cultural fit is a huge piece of what we do. It doesn't matter as much what the qualifications are. If you don't fit the team, you don't fit Rayburn. But of course, there are many ways to fit the team. You can teach skills, but you can't teach personality and character. That's what we're looking for."

The Rayburn Executive Team has discovered that they do not need to be a part of the hiring process of every potential new staff member. They prefer not to be involved unless it is a position that will work directly with them. The standard is to allow the hiring managers and HR to make those decisions because those are the people who will work with the new staff member, and they know what they need. The interview will also have some cross-departmental representation for an unbiased perspective on cultural fit. Then, after the decisions are made, executives will make a point to meet the new hires and welcome them personally.

While the Executive Team trusts the judgment of their hiring managers and HR department in bringing new talent into the organization, they recognize the critical importance of maintaining the company's culture and values throughout the employee lifecycle, including in the way the company handles departures. There is one duty that David Naylor will not delegate, the decision to terminate a position. He believes that this is one part of the job that should always reside with him. Hiring can be a group effort or delegated to the authority of company managers but determining that a Rayburn employee loses the privilege of working with the team is a burden ultimately reserved for the CEO alone. This approach reflects David's leadership style and his deep commitment to the company's culture of integrity and fairness.

As the hub of Rayburn's organizational structure, David recognizes that his actions and decisions have a ripple effect throughout the entire company. By retaining the final say on terminations, he ensures that each case is handled with the utmost care, consideration, and consistency. His personal involvement in the termination process also serves as a powerful reminder of the weight and responsibility that comes with leadership. It reinforces the cultural standard that every employee, regardless of their role or tenure, is a valued member of the Rayburn community and deserves to be treated with dignity and respect, even in the most difficult of circumstances. By shouldering this burden himself, David sets the tone for a culture that prioritizes compassion, accountability, and the well-being of every individual within the organization.

EMBRACE GENERATIONAL DIVERSITY

Leaders at all levels are tasked with staying abreast of local, regional, and national trends if they want to succeed. When a body of research began to emerge in the late 1990s proving the benefits of diversity in the workplace, many large companies and technology giants began considering diversity and inclusion initiatives. This led to diversity and inclusion becoming strategic imperatives in corporate America, culminating in the emergence of chief diversity officers (CDOs) in response to growing diversity in the workplace and society, as well as discrimination and equity issues that were becoming more visible in the public eye.

The rise and fall of these roles was swift in the early 2020s, with conversations focusing largely on race and gender. Smart leaders recognize that many other aspects can, and should, also be considered when working to harness the benefits of a diverse workforce. Research continues to highlight the performance upsides of diversity. People of different educational levels, ages, genders, orientations, abilities, and ethnicities approach problems in different ways with distinct view-points. Homogenous teams can often suffer from groupthink, which means dissenting voices are important to help weigh the pros and cons of any decisions or ideas thoroughly. Teams comprised of people with different perspectives, backgrounds, and experiences tend to develop better solutions because they foster more out-of-the-box thinking. Additionally, a workforce that mirrors your diverse customer base enables better insight into consumer needs and preferences.

For small to mid-size companies, generational diversity often tends to be less than in larger organizations, perhaps because their workforce grows with the company. Start-ups are stereotypically full of fresh-faced young entrepreneurs who can pivot and adapt quickly. These generalizations certainly aren't the rule, of course, but rather trends that seem to emerge over time.

Electric co-ops have been predominantly full of older staff members, who have spent their careers in the same place. David Naylor said, "The electric utility industry is going to struggle over the next five to ten years because around 75 percent of their workforce is going to retire. They have all these older employees, and they have not been very successful at attracting younger people. It's a very mature workforce, and there is a perception that working at a power company is not very interesting or fun."

A key component of Rayburn's growth navigation is to hire to meet the ever-changing needs of the modern marketplace rather than operating as a stale utility stuck in the past. By doing so, Rayburn has positioned itself to attract and retain top talent from younger generations who are less commonly represented in the G&T world. This approach to hiring and managing a workforce aligns with the growing body of research on generational differences in the workplace.

Studies have shown that younger generations, particularly Millennials and Generation Z, have distinct preferences and expectations when it comes to their careers. These employees value purpose-driven work, flexibility, and opportunities for growth and development.[9] They are also more likely to embrace change and innovation and are less likely to be bound by traditional hierarchies and ways of working.[10] Rayburn's focus on culture, collaboration, and innovation creates an environment that appeals to the values and aspirations of this sector of the workforce, an example that can be followed by organizations seeking to bridge the generational divide and build a future-ready workforce.

Rayburn makes a conscious effort to promote generational diversity with the firm belief that people continue to make valuable contributions as they age. David Naylor said, "At Rayburn, we are

9   Ed O'Boyle, "4 Things Gen Z and millennials expect from their workplace," Gallup, March 30, 2021, https://www.gallup.com/workplace/336275/things-gen-millennials-expect-workplace.aspx.

10   Kim Parker, Nikki Graf, and Ruth Igielnik, "Generation Z looks a lot like millennials on key social and political issues," Pew Research Center, January 17, 2019, https://www.pewresearch.org/social-trends/2019/01/17/generation-z-looks-a-lot-like-millennials-on-key-social-and-political-issues/.

looking at the front end of this and doing what everybody else in our industry is going to have to do by bringing in young talent. We're just doing it five to ten years ahead of them, so we're ahead of the curve. We had to do that back in 2017 when eighty-four years' worth of experience walked out the door. We were challenged to really consider who we brought on and how to attract the right people. One of the things we've learned is that younger employees want to work in a place where they feel valued and where they feel they can add value themselves. They want to have some skin in the game."

The Rayburn workforce is extraordinarily diverse in comparison to other co-ops. Individuals are valued for their skills, experiences, and contributions, no matter their age. By bringing together individuals from different age groups, including Baby Boomers, Generation X, Millennials, and Generation Z, Rayburn has reaped the benefits from a rich tapestry of experiences, perspectives, and approaches to work. They aren't afraid to hire straight out of college or to take someone who is a few years from retirement. There is equal potential in both groups.

Additionally, there is far less emphasis on education levels than one might expect. In 2023, nearly half of the organization had no additional education beyond high school. This diversity has fostered a culture of learning and collaboration, where employees are exposed to a wide range of ideas and solutions. As a result, they are better positioned to innovate, adapt to change, and address the complex challenges that occur in today's dynamic business environment. Through de-emphasizing educational status, Rayburn has become a continuous-learning organization where employees are valued for their input and performance.

Generation Shift (%)

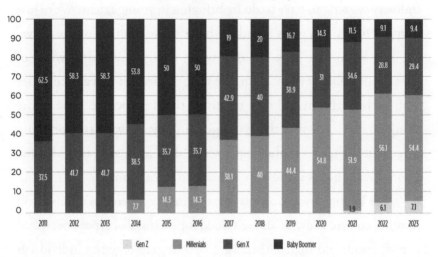

One of the key advantages of generational diversity in any organization is its potential to drive innovation. When employees from different generations work together, they can draw from their unique life experiences and professional backgrounds to solve problems. Younger workers may offer fresh insights into emerging technologies and market trends, while older employees can contribute valuable institutional knowledge and expertise. With distinct values, preferences, and communication styles, each generation represents a unique segment of the consumer market. Furthermore, when employees of all ages feel valued and respected, they are more likely to be engaged and committed to their work. By promoting an inclusive culture that celebrates cross-generational exchange, organizations can foster a sense of belonging which leads to higher levels of employee satisfaction, reduced turnover, and a stronger employer brand.

Scott Donham shared his perspective on age diversity in his team:

> I'm a technical engineer, so prior to coming here, my whole world was wrapped up in "Did I get that widget

80

working correctly." After coming to Rayburn, I had to change that mindset into being proud and excited for my team when we solved problems together.

It helped that we all had the same beliefs about how to approach our work. I was willing to sit under a diesel tank trying to clog something back up because I believe you do it until the job's done. We all are very much go-getters here. Everybody's willing to put on their boots and get out there and get their hands dirty.

If there's a problem, we're going to sit down and figure it out together. I'm not just going to leave you out to dry or try to hold back information, afraid that you're going to take my job if you know everything.

David always stresses to us that we need to make sure that there's room for everyone to grow. People don't want to feel like they are going to be stagnant in the same position for the next twenty years without anywhere to go. We don't want anybody ever to be caught up or left behind because there wasn't a position ready. It's all about giving everyone room to grow without having this hierarchal system with certain percentages that have to be abided by. As a leader at Rayburn, you're empowered to provide input to what the team dynamics should look like.

This kind of attitude is earth-shattering for anyone who comes from a traditional pyramid hierarchy. It can be startling to people who are used to strict protocols and job progression charts. At Rayburn, most of the positions are brand new, so there are no legacy issues to deal with. It's also still relatively small, so everyone has the opportunity to wear multiple hats and customize their professional journey. In a culture like this, there is no place for stale and detrimental stereotypes like Boomers are out of touch, Gen Xers are cynical, and Millennials are entitled. Instead, everyone belongs as long as they care about the work. To keep that culture, Rayburn tries to maintain as little bureaucracy as they can so the focus can be less on age than it is on talent, potential, and most importantly, attitude.

David Naylor elaborates on the reasons behind Rayburn's flat organizational structure. He said, "We've intentionally kept our hierarchy flat because we believe it fosters collaboration, innovation, and a sense of ownership among our employees. When people aren't bogged down by layers of bureaucracy, they're more likely to take initiative, share ideas, and turn to each other to solve problems. With the growth we have experienced, we cannot afford to have it bogged down waiting on me to approve every change. That would become just as frustrating for the employees as it would be for me."

However, maintaining this structure hasn't been without its challenges, especially as the company has grown. "As we've added more people and projects, there's always the temptation to add more layers of management," Naylor admits. "But we've worked hard to resist that urge and find ways to scale our culture alongside our business. It's not always easy, but we believe it's worth the effort to keep our organization as flat and agile as possible."

Rayburn has managed to maintain its flat structure thanks, in part, to investing so heavily in employee development and empowerment. By providing opportunities for cross-functional collaboration, skill-building, and leadership at all levels, the company has been able to distribute decision-making authority and accountability throughout the organization. This approach not only helps keep bureaucracy at bay but also ensures that Rayburn can continue to attract and retain top talent across generations by offering a dynamic and fulfilling work environment.

WORKFORCE ATTITUDE

It's been said that you can fix performance, but you can't fix attitude. Research and workforce experts have long highlighted the significance of prioritizing attitude over experience in the recruitment process. With such disparate demographics joining so quickly, Rayburn was at risk of having a fragmented company. However, because of the hiring emphasis on culture fit, Rayburn employees are startlingly aligned in one crucial aspect: how they view work. Those who join and stay in this company are people who like to work hard, to be challenged, and to push themselves out of their comfort zone. They like that there is no entitlement here and that everyone earns their place.

This isn't just the perception of management. At one point, Rayburn paid for everyone in the company to take a personality assessment that measured natural talents, thinking patterns, and behaviors to see what strengths existed within the company. The results were not at all surprising. David Naylor reported to the Board: "All of our folks like to work hard, be challenged, and tend to be intolerant of those that don't work hard."

He elaborated, "We can't make an argument that we're giving out too much PTO because we're not using very much of it. We have people who like to work, like to work hard, like to be challenged, and don't take breaks. And I'm as bad as anybody. I recognize that. So as we continue to grow though, we've got to be mindful. But this is who we are. I'll admit that one of my concerns is that what we've done at Rayburn has hired a bunch of adrenaline junkies. And as soon as we, as soon as things slow down (of course I don't know when they're going to slow down), we'll find people saying, 'Well, wait a minute. I was here because of the excitement and the pace, and now it's not here.' Will they move on?"

Fair point. But hopefully, with the right attitude, this won't be a problem because the company culture fit will be enough to earn their loyalty.

While Rayburn's culture attracts driven individuals who thrive on challenges, the company also recognizes the importance of work-life balance. Naylor emphasized, "We want our employees to work hard, but we also want them to take time for their families and personal lives. To play hard, too. It's about finding a sustainable balance that allows our team members to perform at their best. Employees should be able to attend parent-teacher conferences, attend sporting events, support spouses' endeavors, and be active in their communities. This makes Rayburn better, and we all benefit."

To support this balance, Rayburn has implemented strategies to shape teams and foster workforce development. By working to create a mix of high-energy innovators and steady, reliable contributors, the company ensures that it has the right blend of skills and personalities to tackle any challenge. Naylor added, "We know that not everyone is wired to be an adrenaline junkie, and that's okay. We value the unique contributions of each team member, whether they're the ones pushing the envelope or the ones ensuring that we stay grounded. It's this diversity of thought and approach that makes the Rayburn team as successful as it is today. It all comes down to attitude."

Skilled and experienced employees with negative attitudes can lead to failure and disruption within any organization. Furthermore, most bad hires are not due to a lack of technical skills but rather due to candidates lacking the right attitudes and mindset. Rayburn isn't the only place that knows this. Employers are increasingly open to hiring candidates with positive attitudes, even if they are not fully qualified for a role. Traits such as optimism, persistence, and fearlessness are highly valued by employers across all industries. When employees maintain the right attitude, it can have a strong effect on productivity and the overall work culture. A positive attitude can influence a company's productivity, reputation, and even its ability to overcome unexpected challenges, such as those posed by the COVID-19 pandemic. On the other hand, a toxic work environment resulting from poor attitudes can lead to high employee turnover and dissatisfaction, ultimately impacting the business negatively.

BEYOND THE JOB DESCRIPTION

A part of the attitude that Rayburn looks for when considering the cultural fit is the willingness to go above and beyond the job description. As Staci Bratcher said, "There aren't a lot of clock watchers around here." The predominant sentiment is that if there is a job to do, you stay until it is done. With the essential nature of the company, coupled with the speed of growth, there is so much to do that it sometimes just can't be accomplished in an eight-hour day.

Stephen Geiger shared his professional journey, which echoes that of many other employees at Rayburn.

> I started off involved with power supply. When I got here, that was really easy because we had a third party who managed our market purchases. Whatever we needed, they gave it to us at a fixed price. But that was rolled off in 2017. I had a few months to get caught up on what that meant to us, including how to buy and sell power within the ERCOT market. Then we had a significant tornado storm come through that decimated our transmission

structures, and I took on more of an operational role. I shifted and moved around so that I now have familiarity with all aspects of the company. Everybody here has had what might amount to a thirty-year career in less than ten. That's the thing about our industry. Everybody here knows they are on call 24/7. For all intents and purposes, everybody's on the clock. When something hits the fan, it's all-hands-on-deck. Even accounting—which you would not think is key to day-to-day operational issues or emergency situations—is still an integral part of the team. We all come in. Everybody knows this is a job that has to get done, so they contribute when it's needed. You can't say, "Well, it's five o'clock, I'm going home." You only check out when the job is done. The mentality that "it's not my problem" doesn't fly around here. If you had that, you wouldn't last because at the end of the day, we all have the same goal, and that is to provide the best service to our Members at the lowest cost. That is incumbent upon everybody at all times. That mentality is ingrained in all of us. We all do our part.

Geiger is an outlier in the industry because he rose to management in his early twenties, where he would routinely find himself in industry meetings where he was the youngest person in the room by decades. Because of the training and support he's received, he was confident in the knowledge and skills he brought to the table, and people found out very quickly that he was not to be dismissed because of his youth. He seized the opportunity for growth offered at Rayburn, and both he and the company have benefited greatly. If he had been at a traditional G&T, he would likely have been told, "Here is where you begin. In two years, you'll be in this part of engineering. Then

86

two years after that, you'll be a lead engineer, and then two years later, you'll be a supervisor. Assuming all goes well, you'll be a manager in ten years." And they would have suffered a huge loss in not being able to have someone of his intelligence, talent, and enthusiasm lead a healthy team.

In other companies, someone who is Gen X, for example, might expect that at one point they will automatically be promoted due to their seniority. That is not the case here. Promotions are based on performance and the embodiment of the values. Are you willing to get your hands dirty and do what has to be done? That will be recognized much more than years on the job.

Rayburn's growth has expanded experience levels and fostered an expectation of advancement among its high-performing employees. This has challenged the Executive Team to create additional opportunities for those employees. Rayburn already recognized that it should encourage its employee base to pursue training opportunities through certifications, seminars, and workshops. Employees are already encouraged to pursue additional education that will be paid for by Rayburn without a requirement or expectation to remain at Rayburn.

The standard at Rayburn is that as long as people continue their growth pattern as contributors, they aren't restricted by their job description. It's open-ended in terms of what value they want to bring to the organization. David Naylor's philosophy is this: "If we do everything we can to support the success of our employees, that will trigger success for the whole company."

If a person depends on a very clearly defined professional path, this is the wrong place for them. This is a place that centers on opportunity for growth, and the company is full of stories of the advantages of espousing this philosophy.

Recently retired CFO David Braun started as controller and took his time learning the business from the ground up. He said, "They actually gave me time every day to read about the industry and what was going on with ERCOT, which was amazing. Somebody asked me about a year after I started how I liked working at a co-op. I said, 'This is the best job I've ever had.'"

Project Coordinator Supervisor Shannon Beber started as a temp accountant and never left. After working in accounting for thirteen years, she was used to the predictability of numbers. But in 2014, she started multitasking in project management simply because there was a need there and she wanted to pitch in. She eventually moved away from accounting to start the project management department and said, "The more we grow, the more this will take on a life of its own. There are so many different aspects that my day is full of now. It's never the same. I love my job. It's so much fun."

And then there's Gentry Ewing, who was hired as the sole Geographic Information System (GIS) employee and is now overseeing an entirely new communications department. He never said, "GIS is my job, and that's all I do." Instead, he was constantly looking for ways where his skills could benefit the company in new ways. The environment motivated him to do things that pushed the boundaries of what a GIS person would normally do, and he was rewarded for that.

The culture of Rayburn has been a constant supply of fuel to serve others, regardless of the project, task, or department. David Naylor and Stephen Geiger decided to approach him to find out what he needed so that he could continue engaging his natural curiosity and talents. "We have a bit of a professional dilemma here," they told him. "We want you to do more than GIS, but we're not entirely sure what that means."

Gentry said, "It would have been so easy to say, 'No. I'm a GIS guy. That's my identity and I'm safe there.' But I didn't. I trusted them more than I trusted myself. I knew they would be able to help me grow. So I agreed to change my role."

They decided to build a role around his skills and asked him to consider first, what that role might look like and second, what he needed to succeed. How many companies offer this kind of freedom to define roles and succeed outside of the confines of a job description?

When it comes to motivating employees to go the extra mile, the freedom to excel is a powerful contributor to an enjoyable and comfortable workplace. This approach not only benefits the business but also helps employees feel more satisfied and engaged in their work. When employees see the bigger picture and understand the impact of their contributions, they are more likely to be motivated to go above and beyond. Is there a manager anywhere who honestly doesn't want to have that?

Gentry said, "The Rayburn culture almost 'pulls you in' naturally. The environment here is extremely motivating, and it surprises you because not everywhere has that DNA. Part of the reason some of us want to give it our all for our fellow team members is because we know they are going to give us the same, if not more, in return. And what happens is others witness it. And then they adopt it. And then that cycle just keeps continuing and staff members gain a newfound confidence to keep pushing the boundaries of what is possible. Instead of trying to force that positive environment into a culture, your employees are helping keep it alive as they understand how motivating and confidence boosting it can be."

As Rayburn has navigated the challenges of rapid growth and a changing workforce, its commitment to culture has remained unwavering. By prioritizing attitude over experience in the hiring process, fostering a flat organizational structure that encourages collaboration and innovation, and embracing the unique strengths of a generationally diverse team, Rayburn has cultivated a work environment that not only attracts top talent but also inspires them to go above and beyond their job descriptions. This has created a team of dedicated, passionate individuals who are united in their pursuit of excellence and their desire to make a meaningful impact. As Rayburn continues to grow and evolve, continued success will undoubtedly be rooted in its ability to maintain this strong cultural foundation while adapting to the ever-changing needs of its employees, Members, and the broader energy landscape. Because of this, Rayburn is firmly positioning itself to face the challenges of the future and emerge as a trailblazer in the cooperative utility sector.

CHAPTER 5

INVESTING IN PEOPLE

If you take care of your employees,
they'll take care of your business.

DAVID A. NAYLOR

An old story has been re-told in various forms on social media and business websites for many years. The author is unknown. It goes something like this:

THE ENGINE MECHANIC[11]

A giant ship's engine failed. The ship's owners hired one expert after another, but none of them could figure out how to fix the engine. The owners were losing money every day as their ship sat idle.

Eventually, they brought in an old timer who had been fixing ships since he was a young man. He carried a large bag of tools with

---

11   Nicholas Cole, "The ship repair man story," Medium, August 6, 2020, https://medium.com/@oceanbcreative/the-ship-repair-man-story-dd959a4469d8.

him, and when he arrived, he immediately went to work, inspecting the engine from top to bottom.

After looking things over, the old man reached into his bag, pulled out a hammer, and reached down and tapped on a small place on the engine. Instantly, the engine sprang back to life. He carefully put his hammer away. The engine was fixed!

A week later, the owners received a bill from the old man for $10,000.

"What?!" the owners exclaimed. "He hardly did anything!"

So they wrote the old man a note saying, "Please send us an itemized bill."

The man sent a bill that read:

Tapping with hammer........................ $2.00
Knowing where to tap.......................... $9,998.00

The moral of the story is probably obvious: while effort is important, wisdom and experience are where value truly lies. In a business context, smart leaders care about finding talented individuals who either already have the wisdom or the right attitude to gain it and will stay with the company long enough to put it to good use. It's up to leaders to find and retain staff members who can bring the metaphorical $10,000 value that the old man brought in the story.

It's one thing to find seasoned talent and another thing entirely to cultivate an atmosphere where wisdom can be created.

FREEDOM TO FIGURE IT OUT

Knowledge and wisdom are not the same thing. As the saying goes, knowledge is knowing that a tomato is a fruit. Wisdom is knowing not to add it to your fruit salad. A person with knowledge carries a full and shiny toolbox full of facts, data, and technical skills gained through study and training. A person with wisdom carries a worn, weathered, and simple toolbox with three tools: awareness, perspective, and good judgment.

As a business leader, it is easy to focus on the skills and knowledge of staff members and forget that what matters most is providing the proper context for the application of those skills and knowledge. Wisdom takes effort, trial and error, and experience. It is gained through action, learning, sharing, and a deep analysis of experiences, both good and bad.

As one example, wisdom dictates that there are occasions when the most compassionate thing one can do is allow another person to suffer. The parent of a toddler knows that a child has to fall down sometimes as they learn to walk. Teachers know that sometimes a student has to get a failing grade to gain the motivation they need to study hard. And good leaders know that sometimes their people have to learn the hard way what to do and what not to do.

"If status quo is not company policy," said David Naylor, "and one of our core values is innovation, then we have to be able to sit back and let our employees have the flexibility to implement the changes they see they need to make without having to go through a whole bureaucracy of approvals. That's why we are a flat organization. Everyone here can evaluate their day-to-day job and ask what they can do to improve, and then try new things. There may be some bumps along the way because of inexperience, but one of the main ways you gain experience is by making mistakes."

Mistakes happen to everyone, and allowing small slip-ups now and then in the workplace can do more good than a host of formal training. Setting an organization-wide tone that mistakes are learning opportunities leads to valuable insights at an individual and company-wide level that will lead to improved performance and a more desirable company culture. Working in an environment where people feel safe trying innovative ideas and taking thoughtful risks is also key for sparking creativity and progress. Setbacks breed resilience over time, helping teams persevere to discover breakthrough solutions.

Chris Anderson said, "We have the core value of excellence. But excellence is not perfection. All of this is inherent in hiring the right people who want to do their jobs well. They don't have their hands held out, wondering what we're going to give them. Instead, they are eager to be trained, and we are eager to grow alongside them."

Workers who know it's alright to make some errors tend to take initiative while also supporting teammates. As long as major errors aren't too frequent or grossly negligent, honest mistakes or failed attempts should not risk ending careers or damaging relationships. Blame-free work cultures build loyalty and trust, bringing people together to solve challenges collaboratively while taking account-ability. Rather than creating a fearful organization that moves slowly to avoid any missteps, embracing mistakes thoughtfully keeps the momentum toward achieving big goals.

In short, if you are a leader hoping to foster this kind of workplace environment, don't sweat the small stuff when it comes to the occasional mistake. Use these moments for growth, have patience as others learn, and focus on progress through resilience. Remind your team that your culture embraces forward motion, not flawlessness. And take time to understand the world your employees live in, as much as you can so that you can appreciate the context of their decision-making. Scott Donham said, "David Naylor gives us the freedom to do what we feel is best. He wants us to bring ideas. It helps that he's an electrical engineer because when my group is bringing new ideas, he's not going to question everything like a business guy would. He understands the engineering side of what we're trying to do."

There is no such thing as a perfect organization. There are no perfect people. But creating an environment where talented staff can thrive is the key to success for visionary leaders.

TURNING A INTO A+

Gentry Ewing said, "It's one thing to find an all-star, but they won't stay that way for long if they don't have the tools, resources, and atmosphere they need to do their job well. Our goal is to find 'A' talent and figure out how we can help them become 'A+.'" The key is providing a supportive and growth-oriented environment. The most obvious and common way is by providing opportunities for continuous improvement and learning for staff members.

Savvy leaders know that decisions can't be based on how easy or hard the choice is; they have to make choices based on what the anticipated impact of that decision will be. In typical organizations, leaders begin by identifying areas for growth, setting specific goals, and seeking feedback from those working on the ground. They analyze the return on investment (ROI) on training costs, including curriculum development, instructional design, venue rentals, instructor fees, technology, and employee time away from actually performing their jobs. Then, they look at the payback period before those costs are justified by recouping the investment in value to the bottom line. There is an ROE for this as well—return on expectation. The nonfinancial benefits include greater team unity, increased job satisfaction, higher morale, and greater loyalty. People tend to stay where they feel they belong, where they are needed, and where they can contribute in meaningful ways.

A company can't hope to turn "A" talent into "A+" talent if they can't first retain them. By nurturing a holistic approach to personal and professional growth, leaders improve retention rates dramatically. It's one thing to offer competitive benefits, recognizing individual achievements, and foster continuous learning and development. It is another thing to create an environment where staff members feel they belong.

Rayburn is still tinkering and learning the best ways to promote and support all of their staff members in the best ways, and it all starts with the approach they take to training. If you want to follow the Rayburn way, constant and open communication is where it all begins. Check in regularly with employees about their professional goals and aspirations. Then, actively invest in skill development through coaching, training programs, stretch assignments, and support for continuous learning. Demonstrate paths forward. Make yourself accessible for dialogue through open office hours, small group lunches/meetups, surveys on the employee experience, and an open-door policy. Welcome constructive input, acknowledge concerns, and follow up on suggestions or issues raised.

Avoid excessive overtime expectations. Accommodate flexibility in schedules/locations when possible. Support activities unrelated to work and encourage paid time off. Understand obligations outside work. Show value for personal health and family commitments comes first. Anticipate and mitigate, don't react.

This approach has so far proven successful. Perhaps more telling is the fact that Rayburn's people routinely report that they feel like they are a part of a family. This tone is set by the Board Chairman, David McGinnis: "We are a family. The co-op is a family." And that tone resonates throughout the Rayburn organization. Chris Anderson said:

It sounds cliché for me to say that Rayburn has a family atmosphere. But when you think about the genesis of the co-op business model and the necessity in the 1930s to electrify rural areas through a cooperative effort of similarly-situated farmers and rural Americans, you actually do feel the family theme flow from that beginning to current-day business operations. I came to Rayburn after twenty-seven years at an investor-owned electric utility, so I have a unique perspective and have seen the Wall Street side of the electric utility business. Here, we are supplying our Members with electricity that serves their friends, neighbors—people they know and are in contact with every day. Layer on top of that the fact that many of the employees of those co-ops have mothers or fathers who also worked in those co-ops. Electric co-ops and other utilities are unique in terms of long-term employment. You begin to understand the reference and resonance of a family atmosphere. Now fast forward to today's Rayburn: we may come from different backgrounds, but we come together for the common goal that Rayburn strives for every day to serve its four Member cooperatives so they can serve their families and friends. The co-op governance model permeates how we operate and how we serve. It cannot help but reinforce the culture and the family aspect of Rayburn.

Rayburn places a great deal of importance on offering meaningful work experiences designed to improve employee engagement, to provide opportunities for challenging and impactful projects, and to allow ownership.

"RIGHT" TRAINING

While it is better to offer some formal learning options than none, providing the right training is key to avoiding disengagement, imprecise budget allocations, and failure to build essential workforce capabilities and atmosphere. Thoughtful design, validation, and intentionality in training pays dividends.

There are several potential risks associated with providing the wrong type of training to employees. The most obvious is that gaps will remain unaddressed if training does not match the core skills employees actually need to fulfill their roles, performance won't measurably improve, and capability problems will persist. It is also a waste of time and resources if the training has limited relevance or doesn't translate into individual and/or business impact. It diminishes that all-important ROI.

On a more personal level, employees can become de-motivated and disengaged if they perceive training to be a compliance checklist item instead of truly advancing their goals or performance. Or, they may feel pulled in too many directions if pieces of training focus on ancillary factors rather than aligning tightly to their personal and professional goals, diluting the value of the training.

Training doesn't always have to take the form of a formal sit-down, hours-long, instructor-led experience with a formal curriculum. Rayburn finds that some of the most meaningful and beneficial training comes in the form of simple, informal, one-on-one conversations.

Employee engagement increases when an employee feels better connected to the purpose behind their work. Instead of an accountant crunching numbers or an IT administrator patching a server, Rayburn takes the time to show staff members what impact these tasks have for the company and the Members. It's not just another Excel book or another server. It becomes part of the overall mission and commitment to what Rayburn was created to do and empowers employees to bring greater value every day.

Thanks to the flat organizational setup, Rayburn allows managers to test ideas out in their departments without having to get prior approval. For example, even though Scott Donham is the Engineering Manager, he felt that it was important to take the accounting team on a trip to explore the operations side of the company. Erica Hilton was one of the accountants who went. She said, "We're paying bills for all these pieces and parts, and we don't know what we're looking at. Scott walked us through and said, 'Here's a breaker. Here's a V Switch. This is a cable trench.' All I ever saw before that was words on paper, but after he took time out of his day to give us that tangible experience, I know what they mean now."

The investment in that kind of training was minimal—a few hours, but the return was great. Those accountants can attach real meaning to their paperwork and, in all likelihood, will be better able to catch potential errors. Informal training experiences like this can be crucial for organizations that want to keep up with rapidly changing workplace demands. This type of fluid, less structured development addresses evolving employee and organizational needs in real time. Rather than being an ad hoc add-on to the existing training curriculum, flexible ongoing informal experiences enhance formal learning programs, allowing companies to nurture talent and maintain a workforce capable of meeting contemporary workplace challenges.

BREAKFAST CLUB

Focused, ongoing training emerged naturally from Rayburn's culture of questioning the status quo. In 2021, David Naylor and the other executives began to wonder if some staff members were not being given sufficient opportunities to fully develop their potential. Several staff members were identified who consistently contributed above and beyond their job description, and leadership began to question what more could be done to give these specific employees a chance to shine in a new way.

An idea emerged out of a desire to be more intentional about providing intensive leadership training to these top performers for the benefit of these individuals and for the company. At an off-site strategy session, the Executive Team brainstormed topics that could be further explored, including communication, company culture, agility, decision-making, and team resilience. They knew that adding yet another demand on an already busy team presented several risks. If not approached in the right way, it could easily be just a box to check, do it, and move on, with little actual change made. It could also be the proverbial straw that broke the camel's back—bogging down these go-getters to the point of being overwhelmed.

To avoid this, they decided to invite a small cadre of participants as a trial run. The idea was to meet monthly for eight months for ninety minutes in the morning, before the workday started. A proud Gen Xer, Naylor decided to call it the "Breakfast Club." Eight people were chosen from the list of those who had displayed noticeable leadership potential in their positions, intentionally selected from different departments.

Each of these people received a formal invitation:

Congratulations (or, after you read this, condolences)! You are part of a small group of employees that have been selected to participate in the inaugural Rayburn Breakfast Club.

Rayburn's vision is to be the pre-eminent G&T in the nation. We strongly believe that developing our employees is a key component to achieving that vision. Our Breakfast Club is a boots on the ground initiative to put action to our belief.

The purpose of the Breakfast Club is to (1) educate you on the business of Rayburn and (2) challenge and grow you in your professional development.

We are asking you for a ten-month commitment. During this time, there will be eight monthly meetings—7:00 to 8:30 AM (Yes, that is AM).

August 26, 2021	February 24, 2022
September 23, 2021	March 24, 2022
October 28, 2021	April 28, 2022
January 22, 2022	May 26, 2022

Each Breakfast Club participant will be assigned to a team. The team will complete homework assignments and present them to the full group. All of this will culminate into a captone presentation.

We understand not everyone will be able to make the required commitment, but we hope that you will give this opportunity a strong consideration.

We invite you to attend the kick-off meeting on August 26 at 7:00 AM. Be prepared to discuss these four questions:

- Why did you choose Rayburn?
- Why have you stayed at Rayburn?
- What do you want from Rayburn?
- What strengths do you bring to Rayburn? (Refer to your strength finders results and reach out to us if you do not have them.)

Please RSVP to us by July 30, 2021.

Unsurprisingly, everyone who was invited accepted the invitation and came to the first meeting prepared as requested in the invitation. They received the curriculum at this initial meeting, so they could better understand what was expected of them. Gentry Ewing was in that first group, and he said, "It was a commitment, but we had full trust in the Executive Team and wanted to take advantage of this great opportunity."

These monthly meetings are intense. Each participant is required to complete homework and come prepared to work with their designated team toward a capstone project. Regular presentations are a part of the experience, which is enough to make some participants anxious. Erica Hilton was a part of the second Breakfast Club. She said:

> When you speak on something you're an expert on, that's comfortable. But here we're talking about building battery storage stations and trying to present on that. It was very difficult for me. I have an Apple Watch and at the end of my first Breakfast Club executive presentation was over, I went back to my desk. My watch said that my heart rate had been above 120 beats per minute for more than ten minutes. I took a picture of it and sent it to David Braun with a note that said, "I was almost in cardiac arrest. This club is crazy!"

This training opportunity upholds the core value of excellence as it provides participants the chance to rise. They see that leaders are not stingy with their knowledge. It is available to all. People like Erica, who was happy to keep her head down in accounting, realize that they might have more in them than they thought. If the CEO sees potential, there must be potential there, which is hugely encouraging. Graduates of the Breakfast Club improve the talent pool that the Executive Team sees as the next generation of leaders at Rayburn.

The strategic effort to invite participants from different departments serves to also cross-pollinate the organization. These frontline staff members are the "team of teams" that the Rayburn Executive Team relies upon to help spread messages as well as garner feedback from employees. So, within the flat organizational structure, Rayburn has developed its own amorphous structure that can be utilized as the company grows. Participants gain a better understanding of what matters to their coworkers and how problem solving can be approached from new perspectives. The value of having someone from IT, for example, who might look at a computer screen all day, get out and mingle in a meaningful way with operations, accounting, and legal, means that they can listen to all aspects of the business and understand their role in a greater context. It opens eyes. It builds trust. They are asked to be a team and accomplish real work, doing some of the legwork of the Executive Team, which adds tremendous value to the individuals and the company as a whole. "If you truly want to be successful at your work, you need to learn the business and not just your job," David Naylor said.

ONGOING EDUCATION

Evidence that Rayburn actually does listen to its people is the fairly recent addition of education reimbursement to the company policy. If the education, certificate, or degree makes sense to the company, employees will get reimbursed for seeking that 100 percent. This grew from a suggestion that came up in Breakfast Club as an honest question, and after careful consideration, it just made sense to add that as an option to enhance the Rayburn culture.

David Naylor said, "If we have hired someone who is a cultural fit, we can always help them get the skills they need to do their job well. This includes helping them get certifications and degrees if they want. If it's a continued education credit or more training so they can get licensed, we support that. If they want to sit for their CPA or PE or any other certificate, we encourage that. That's just part of the investment we make in our employees."

There are no handcuffs attached to the type of training that people can seek, as long as it makes sense to the company, all the way up to a PhD. Chase Snuffer said, "It's nice that we aren't limited in what we want to do. Let's say that you're an IT person, but you want to move into accounting. Not a problem. Or if you're an accountant who wants to be an engineer or an attorney. As long as it's pertainable to Rayburn, go ahead. It's all about finding people who are good at something and letting them spread their wings."

While educational reimbursement may not be that unusual in the corporate world, the way Rayburn approaches it is unique. Most organizations require people to agree to stay with the company for a certain period of time or reimburse the cost of the education to return the company's investment in those educational hours. Not at Rayburn. David Naylor said, "We're not investing in the company. We're investing in our people, so we can't get complacent. We have to make sure that we're taking care of our employees and encouraging them. If we can't keep them here, then shame on us. It's up to us to create a culture that keeps them."

EMPLOYEE ENGAGEMENT

At Rayburn, employee engagement is the second-most important focus of the work, right behind supporting the Members. Engagement is about the dynamic flow of ideas that give purpose a pulse. Team members who are energized by and invested in a shared mission become naturally motivated to do their best work in service of the team's success. It feels easier to think creatively, collaborate, and take initiative instead of going through the motions. Pride and passion together fuel the motivation to keep learning, keep improving, and keep discovering new ways to make positive impacts. Team members are transformers in their own right—elevating their roles, amplifying their impact, and distributing their innovation across the organization.

In contrast are the all-too-common toxic workplaces ruled by disengaged auto-pilot team members simply checking boxes and losing motivation by the minute under the shadow of uninspiring leadership. It's hard to feel that intrinsic reward when progressing toward unclear goals or misaligned priorities. No matter how talented individuals may be, a disengaged group won't sustain high performance. No level of free snacks or ping pong tables masks echoes of indifference, frustration, and lack of trust for long. It's a realm where talent remains tethered by the weight of unclear goals and the gravity of misaligned priorities. A place where even the most skilled individuals become mired in mediocrity.

Scott Donham said, "It's all about the upfront expectations here at Rayburn. It is a lot of fun to do things with people here because everybody really does seem to enjoy the ability to work without a micromanager. We're not sitting here dreading things. I want to have their back the same way that management has mine."

By truly investing in every individual's growth and fulfillment at work, managers reap tenfold returns through heightened agility, innovation, and ambassadorship from their energized team. When people feel activated by purpose (beyond a paycheck) as valued members of a high-performing crew, their satisfaction gets unleashed in countless positive externalities.

An engaged workforce is a strategic asset that delivers returns at multiple levels. When employees feel that they belong and are a part of something greater than themselves, they tend to be more driven, productive, and willing to go the extra mile. Employee engagement boosts morale, retention, innovation, productivity, service quality, and even financial performance. At Rayburn, there are several ways that employees are invited to become more engaged, including Let's Connect events and other company-wide celebrations.

LET'S CONNECT EVENTS

Similar to many corporations, Rayburn has annual celebrations like company picnics and Christmas parties, but what staff members talk about most are the "Let's Connect" events. Also like many companies, Rayburn has a team to determine employee activities. Here, it's called the EAT (employee activity team). They plan and host these monthly events where every person in the company is invited to come and interact for an hour or so in the afternoon. These activities have included catered meals, games, and competitions such as corn hole, gingerbread house building, board games, chili cook-offs, trivia, and Halloween costume contests. Prizes are awarded and sometimes rotated through the office like a coveted wooden paddle given annually for the fastest crawfish eater. These regular get-togethers foster a sense of belonging and unity, where they can switch off the work responsibilities for a moment and be real people.

Stephen Geiger said, "We spend so much time with each other. You want to like the people you work with. We all take a great amount of pride in this. It isn't just, 'You're my coworker and I don't want anything to do with you after five.' Rayburn does a great job putting together events where we get to know each other better and do things that help us leave work at our desks for a little while."

This level of connection yields tangible benefits. Employees gain work friends and even recommend jobs to people in their personal networks because of the welcoming environment. Perhaps most importantly, the interactions boost employee engagement. When people feel invested in their colleagues and enjoy being around them, they take more satisfaction in their work. Rayburn's efforts to unite people across divisions, roles, and backgrounds is an example of leading with empathy. The successes speak for themselves—happy, loyal teams doing their best work together.

Luke Jones, a transmission substation superintendent, said, "Yes, we all have a job to do, and we have to get our job done, but there's also that time for entertainment. Rayburn cares about what we do and how we feel. It's not just a 'Let's Connect' where we come for the cookies and ice cream. It's the fellowship. They ask me about my kids. I ask them about their kids. Even though we're from totally different backgrounds, all of that is pushed to the side, and you have that sense of family with people that you would probably never interact with in your life. If I'm here on campus, which is not very often, I'll stop and talk to people for ten, or fifteen minutes, and make my rounds.

And the same thing if we're in the warehouse and they come through, they make a point to stop and talk to us. I've got people that I'm close with outside of Rayburn now gotten jobs here. They all say the same thing. We do the line and substation work. We're the dirty, grungy guys. And we may come in and be filthy, but we're not looked down upon. I mean it truly is family."

Ultimately, the company's emphasis on nurturing interpersonal relationships enhances engagement, unity, and the overall employee experience. Without this kind of camaraderie, employees might as well be independent contractors.

In today's fast-paced corporate world, organizations must prioritize the happiness and well-being of their employees to attract and retain top talent. Cultivating joy in the workplace is essential for creating a positive and productive work environment. Joy encourages a culture centered on relationships, meaningful work, value, and fulfillment. It can also lead to a stronger work ethic, increased motivation, and a more engaged workforce. Fostering joy in the workplace is not just a nice-to-have element; it is a practical and science-based approach that can have a profound impact on both employee well-being and organizational success.

There are big-screen televisions situated right where most of the foot traffic happens on the Rayburn campus. They announce new hires, work anniversaries, birthdays, and other causes for celebration. When people walk by, they see a picture, a name, and the reason for recognition. It's a simple way to help the company feel even more connected.

FUN IN THE WORKPLACE

The electric industry is a serious business. Electric utilities provide a crucial service, and the stakes are high. If people at the end of the line are without power, there can be dire consequences, so the fun and joy have to be kept within the proper bounds. Linemen working on a 138,000-volt line until 3:00 a.m. do not have the time for Nerf guns; they are in a lock-step process where everyone is laser-focused on their tasks, with no room for error.

You don't get hired at Rayburn if you aren't willing to work hard. Stephen Geiger said, "It's an important balance. I'm not going to lie. We are really busy. We do a lot of work here. So we work hard, but then we play hard. You bust your tail doing whatever needs to be done, and then you can have fun. The last thing I want you to do if you're on my team is get burned out."

Against this backdrop stands Rayburn's testament: a workplace thrumming with the zest of autonomy and the harmony of trust. The dividends reaped from nurturing every individual's growth are manifold: agility, innovation, and ambassadorship. These are the returns on an investment in a workplace where being engaged and energized by purpose transcends the mere transactional nature of work. Here, satisfaction is not confined—it's a force unleashed, spreading its positive charge through every aspect of the organization.

Having fun is just as much a part of the Rayburn fabric. Chase Snuffer might take his IT team to the bowling alley. Scott Donham had his team leave work early one Friday to play disc golf at a local park. They didn't talk about work or projects. It was about laughing, having a good time, and improving their relationships. These out-of-office moments do a world of good in terms of improving team morale.

In the office, the environment is joyful. Laughter is heard in the hallways. Practical jokes are the norm. Sara Richard teased someone about playing Christmas music in November and arrived to work the next day to find her entire office wrapped in Christmas wrapping paper—walls, computer, chair, everything. When the company purchased the power generation plant called Panda Sherman, the announcement came from a mystery man wearing a giant panda costume (the head of which now sits with pride in Chris Anderson's office). When the Executive Team moved out to a temporary portable while the campus was under construction, someone put fake legs with ruby slippers poking out as though it had landed on top of the Wicked Witch of the East. And the Executive Team all have Nerf guns on their desks.

David Naylor said of the guns, "I made a comment about how nice it would be to have a Nerf gun in my office once, and all of a sudden, Amazon shows up with some. I said, 'Well, as long as I have the biggest ammo, OK. I'm not going to be outgunned.'"

Scott Donham added, "It's all in good fun. You might be sitting in your office, really deep in thought and suddenly somebody pops in and starts shooting you with a Nerf gun. It helps relieve that stress and reminds you that you have to laugh and have a good time too. Don't take yourself so seriously."

The secret to success in all of this is knowing how to walk that balance. Wise leaders tend to have high emotional intelligence, which includes being self-aware and understanding personal values as well as the values of others. They know when to laugh and when not to laugh. They know how to create opportunities for other team members to mentor and guide, thereby passing on their wisdom and experience to their colleagues. They encourage risk-taking and create an environment where team members can learn from their failures. And most importantly, they don't force it.

Erica Hilton observed, "This is a place of constant creativity and movement, true to the way Rayburn invests in their employees and the way we invest in each other. Everyone is authentic because we're allowed to be authentic. They don't put a cork in all of this. It's not like, 'You're an accountant, you're supposed to be quiet. Go in there and pay some bills. Sit at your computer. Don't raise your head.' Mr. Naylor gave me a Nerf gun because he wanted me to pick people off coming around the corner. It's fantastic. They are all approachable and real. They're not somebody who's on Mahogany Row. We're trusted with our own jobs, and we have the potential to grow in any direction. We encourage and uphold our values and integrity. And we're still silly and inappropriate, and we haze each other and there's a lot of hallway fun. But it's fun and kindness."

CHAPTER 6

WHY WE CARE

Principles mean your decisions are already made for you.

DAVID A. NAYLOR

Darren Hardy's book *The Compound Effect* examines the powerful amplifying impact of small, smart choices accumulated over time and outlines key lessons on how to harness the exponential snowball effect of self-improvement. One example that he uses is that of the Compounding Penny.

If you were given a choice between $3 million or a penny that doubled every day for a month, which would you choose? Many people would want the $3 million because it seems ridiculous that a penny could grow in a month to be more than that.

Simple math answers this quickly. In a day, the penny has doubled. It becomes four, then eight, then sixteen. Pretty dreary compared to millions, right? Twenty days in, and you have $5,000 which is nice, but when you think about that compared to $3 million, it's still pretty pathetic.

But at twenty-nine days, you have $2.7 million, then $5.3 million, and then on the very last day of the month, you wake up to $10,737,418.24. A single penny, the smallest coin, can be the start of something great.

THE COMPASS OF CORE VALUES

In the fabric of Rayburn's operations, the four simple core values act as a compass for all decisions, emphasizing truth, character, and the pursuit of ideas: Integrity, Respect, Excellence, and Innovation. These values are more than simple guidelines. They are the essential tenets from which all decisions are made. Roy Disney said, "It's not hard to make decisions once you know what your values are." As always, Rayburn takes that wisdom and pushes it a step further. As David Naylor said, "Principles mean your decisions are already made for you."

For instance, if a person has a principle of prioritizing honesty, they don't need to spend time debating whether to tell the truth in a particular situation. Their principle has already made the decision for them. This saves time, energy, and mental resources, allowing them to focus on more important matters. The same can be said of companies.

Any organization seeking to navigate the complexities of today's business environment effectively will have defined core principles that are foundational in decision-making. These values are not just words on a page but are lived experiences and truths that define the character of the organization. In the vast sea of challenges and opportunities that modern businesses face, having these firmly set will provide direction, ensure consistency in decision-making, and foster a culture of integrity and purpose.

Consistently emphasizing these principles throughout the organization as a guide for decision-making also reinforces a sense of unity and shared purpose among employees. It cultivates a culture where everyone understands what the organization stands for, leading to a more cohesive and motivated workforce. This shared understanding is crucial for maintaining a positive and productive work environment, especially in times of change or adversity.

Having a foundation focus provides resilience and adaptability because predetermined values provide leaders with the wisdom and space to navigate crises with the confidence to adapt without compromise.

Having a set of core principles as a compass is not just beneficial; it is essential for any organization aiming for long-term success and impact. The Rayburn moral compass of Integrity, Respect, Excellence, and Innovation manifests in three distinct behaviors: truth-telling, the relentless pursuit of ideas and innovation, and character.

At Rayburn, truth is the keystone that holds the company together. In a world full of sycophants and pleasers, truth-telling fosters transparency, resilience, and trust. Truth is what reputations are built on, both inside and without the walls of any organization. It illuminates the path forward through growth stages and ensures that every decision aligns with the organization's mission and vision. But it can't be just lip service. If you claim that you value truth as a leader, you cannot shy from it, even if (perhaps especially if) truth is uncomfortable to hear. It must be invited, welcomed, and acted upon. Growth can only happen after you first acknowledge where you are and that there is always room to grow. This is how Rayburn ensures that its character remains unassailable. This is how Rayburn maintains its high ethical standards and integrity in all its dealings.

This philosophy is how Rayburn's innovative spirit has been allowed to thrive. When leaders remain firmly open to truth, they establish trust in open communication, setting the stage for curiosity to develop because the bar for reprimand or rejection is taken down. Rayburn's humble and cooperative nature has instilled a commitment among all its staff to exploration. It also encourages that all-important culture of excellence, where new ideas are not just welcomed but are actively sought out and tested.

This openness and collective pursuit of excellence are not present only under the gaze of observation, to impress the managers. They are evident in the absence of scrutiny as well. Former UCLA basketball coach John Wooden's profound insight into character echoes within the walls of Rayburn, "The true test of a man's character is what he does when no one is watching."

Character is not just an attribute at Rayburn; it is a priority. It is the sieve through which all actions are filtered, ensuring that the cooperative's operations are not just effective, but that they are ethically sound and aligned with long-term goals. This focus on character has cemented Rayburn's reputation as a trustworthy and reliable entity in the energy sector, capable of making tough decisions with grace and dignity.

Here, the measure of integrity does not have to be showcased in grand gestures but in the quiet, consistent actions taken when the corridors are empty and the offices, silent. Here, in the unseen corners of effort and decision-making, lies the true testament of Rayburn's spirit, as leaders and staff alike uphold the values of honesty and innovation, regardless of witness or accolade. In the quiet moments, away from the public eye, Rayburn's true character shines brightest.

Whether it's meticulously maintaining the integrity of their transmission lines across rural expanses or innovating within their smart grid technology without immediate acclaim, Rayburn's commitment to excellence and service does not waver. The work that goes into keeping the lights on often happens in the shadows of public attention, but nobody at Rayburn seems to mind. They don't do it for praise or awards. They do it to ensure reliability and efficiency for the Members. This dedication underscores the profound sense of responsibility that guides Rayburn's every decision and action, marking the true measure of their character.

For Rayburn, this compass has been a guiding light through times of calm and storm alike, ensuring that its course remains true to its mission of service, innovation, and community engagement. As Rayburn continues to navigate the future, its compass of core principles will undoubtedly continue to be its most valuable navigational tool. These are the long-term, foundational motivations behind Rayburn's deep-rooted commitment to serving and contributing to the community of Rockwall and beyond.

SPARKING THE HEART OF SERVICE

Generosity has a cascading impact by inspiring others to also show empathy, care, and kindness within their own circles. It taps into our human interconnectivity and ability to exponentially uplift each other.

This is where a concept that David Naylor calls "the art of the important" comes in. Certain lines in the sand get drawn according to your values and principles. As you grow and mature in your career, you start to see and understand the big picture and how certain decisions play in the overall scheme. As part of your leadership growth, you begin to see how something important to an employee might not be very important to the overall picture of your organization. Rather than crush that employee's spirit, leaders learn how to build them up and give them a sense of pride by approving their request. These relatively minor factors may not be very important to the big picture of the entire company, but it is immensely important to that person.

The art of the important requires leaders to strike a delicate balance between the needs and enthusiasm of the individual and the needs of the organization. It means communicating to your people that "What matters to you matters to me because you matter to me." By taking the time to understand the nuances of their priorities and finding ways to accommodate requests whenever possible, leaders can do wonders for developing a culture of trust and respect.

There are other ways to live the "art of the important." Nick O. Rowe takes this principle a step further in his book *The Goodwill Jar*.

> When people come to you and they are excited, let them have it. Maybe it's their first house, first car, first baby, whatever. So many times I have seen leaders take people's joy by saying something like, "I remember my first house," or "I was excited just like you when I bought my first Mercedes." That one-upping kind of talk robs people of their excitement.
>
> This takes away from the joy of the moment. Don't be a joy-stealer. Instead, give joy freely. Generosity will bring the joy. So does accepting the generosity of others. Let others do things for you. Don't insult them when they offer you of their time, their money, their love. When you are generous, that can sometimes create an imbalance, so it is good to let others share their gifts.
>
> In leadership roles, you have to be generous with your time and your grace. It's best to let others come to decisions on their own, even if you know a better way. They may get to the same place in their own way, and you don't have to make it about you and your way. You shouldn't rob that experience from them. And sometimes

their way turns out to be better than what you thought it would. Figuring things out on our own brings joy.

Rayburn cares deeply about its people. Just as much as it cares about keeping the lights on. "We all want to work for a company that matters," said David Braun. "We fully appreciate just how much electricity matters."

A huge part of Rayburn's success lies in its profound understanding of what really matters. It is not limited to the superficial layers of monetary rewards or titles. Instead, it is most often found through connection and community. This is why Rayburn has such a well-established history of service. Rayburn's dedication to community service is not just a part of its operational strategy; it is a reflection of its core identity. This commitment is manifested through a variety of initiatives, from grants and contributions to local engagement activities, illustrating Rayburn's profound connection to the communities where it operates.

Performing acts of service for others cultivates purpose and meaning. It builds and strengthens relationships and deepens understanding between both sides. It counters individualism with the spirit of contributing to something bigger than oneself. A culture of service creates a community with shared purpose and values.

Service gives people an avenue to devote their time and energy toward making a positive difference in the lives of others. It taps into higher ideals of compassion, contribution, and selflessness, which drives personal growth. Volunteering develops empathy, expands perspectives, builds skills, and promotes personal growth. Both collective and grassroots efforts fueled by service can elevate individuals and tackle root causes that contribute to many social problems.

Simply put, service improves lives. What we give, how we share our talents, and how we lift each other all have a compounding effect.

A commitment to service speaks to some of the highest principles of human potential—to connect, to grow, to find meaning and purpose, and to raise each other up. Its impacts ripple outward, strengthening bonds and bettering the world.

Rayburn actively works to engage with the broader community outside the boundaries of business. Staff members have a habit of watching for needs around them, and then trying to fill those needs. This is due, in large part, to the fact that the type of people Rayburn attracts are hard-working, driven, and charitable anyway.

Many companies have a charitable contributions fund, and Rayburn is no different. A team is appointed to identify organizations and groups within the communities they serve that could use additional support. Erica Hilton is one of the members of this team. She said, "Rayburn genuinely wants to impact the communities we serve, and not just with charitable contributions. The things Rayburn does to give back to the community are unbelievable. How the Executive Team finds the time to support all of the things we do is beyond me. It all starts at the top. It's not just lip service. These guys come out to the events and participate alongside us. They walk that walk."

Rayburn's engagement in the community is characterized by active participation and support for local initiatives. This involvement goes beyond mere monetary donations, reflecting a deeper commitment to the community's overall well-being and resilience. By addressing local needs and supporting community projects, Rayburn plays a crucial role in building stronger, more vibrant communities. This engagement not only enhances Rayburn's reputation but also builds trust and strengthens relationships with community members and local organizations.

Erica described one service effort the company participated in. "There is a children's shelter in a nearby community. Rayburn held a food drive to support the shelter for one year. Now, we're a highly competitive culture here, in a good way. When you pit people here against each other, big things happen. We all have a moving box in our departments, with the challenge that the first to fill the box wins the competition. I think my team filled three boxes."

The Executive Team allocated a corporate match, which, when combined with the cash donations from staff members, was used to get backpacks for each of the children who came through the shelter. Erica went on, "When they're taken out of their homes, they have nothing. Maybe a little grocery sack with a few things. When we found that out, we all pulled together again and donated little rollout beds so they could have little nap beds for movie night."

It was no surprise to the HR department who collected the donations each day that this drive went far better than they ever could have expected. This habit of going above and beyond to fill needs is commonplace, and they have a reputation for being the ones to call when help is needed. An elementary school near the Rayburn corporate campus called Staci Bratcher in HR out of the blue one day and said they were having a field trip to a swimming pool. Twenty of their kids had families who were not in a financial position to buy swimming suits. Staci asked what sizes they needed and left the office right away to go buy those suits and delivered them before the field trip started that day. The kids were able to fully participate because, as Erica said, "There's not a lot of red tape, so we can do things like that. We have the freedom to help."

Rayburn also has a long history of supporting charitable causes through grants and contributions. Rayburn demonstrates a proactive approach to supporting initiatives that align with its mission of energy efficiency, sustainability, and community welfare. These contributions are tangible expressions of Rayburn's dedication to fostering a better world beyond its immediate business interests.

Community service provides any organization that chooses to prioritize it with opportunities to connect with community members, local organizations, and other stakeholders. These relationships foster collaboration, partnerships, and mutual support, which are essential for the long-term success of both the cooperative and the community. Through these efforts, any company can not only contribute to the overall community's well-being but also strengthen its own internal culture and identity.

TAKE CARE OF WHAT MATTERS MOST

It's all well and good to donate money and time to children's shelters and elementary schools, but if your people aren't taken care of as well, the charitable heart is not complete. Rayburn considers the health and well-being of its people to be of crucial importance.

Life events are recognized and celebrated. If an employee has a baby, meals are sent from the company. Same thing if someone has to have surgery and is in recovery. Or if they experience the loss of a loved one. They are keenly aware that as they grow, it could be easy to lose sight of what makes Rayburn so great.

Erica Hilton has been a volunteer coach for the local children's soccer league for fifteen years. One spring, she found out that the recreation trailer was stolen along with all of the equipment needed for the kids to practice and play. She received a group email from the director of the organization asking everyone to dig around at home and bring whatever they had.

Because she trusted and respected her employer, she forwarded the email to David Naylor, who immediately donated a sum of money to help the league get set up again. It is worth noting that any employee who wants to volunteer in the community is given flexibility in their schedule to do so.

What matters to you matters to us. That is the silent message that permeates every event and meeting. One remarkable example is the way that they approach the company Christmas party. A few years ago, David Naylor came into Staci's office and said, "You know, I've been thinking ..."

Staci thought, "Oh boy, here we go."

He went on to reflect on past Christmas parties. They had brought in a Santa and a photographer to go with the delicious catered meals. The setting was always lovely, decorated with all the lights and colors of the season. But there was an opportunity that hadn't been explored yet.

"What if we had Santa give gifts to the kids?" David asked.

Staci thought back to that conversation and shared her thoughts:

> My team knows that we are always looking through the lens of, "What can we do to provide an exceptional employee experience?" It's not enough just to be good; if you think about our core values of excellence, we have to ask, "What can we do to provide an exceptional employee experience?" What do we do that shows that we care about you and we care for your family? We want your family to come to the Christmas party and have a phenomenal time.
>
> And so I told my team, "We are not going to get generic gifts. We are going to get gifts they actually want, and gifts that are different from each other." I did not want

one kid to show up and we would go, "Oh, so sorry, we don't have a gift."

We wrapped everything and put gift tags with each child's name on them and had Santa hand each child their own unique gift. This is just one way we are always looking at how we can make things better.

The essence of Rayburn's philosophy reveals a deep-seated belief in the power of community, and their history is a testament to the cooperative commitment to extend a caring reach beyond the confines of any single office. By fostering a culture of volunteerism, Rayburn transcends the mere act of corporate giving and works to nurture a better society. Its dedication to this cause is woven into the fabric of every action, every gesture of support—big or small—affirming that at Rayburn, taking care of what matters most isn't just a statement; it's a living, breathing part of the cooperative's identity. This is the kind of legacy that doesn't just build a business; it builds a family, it strengthens a community, and it creates a lasting impact that resonates with every life it touches.

PATHWAY TO YES

One of the many unique phrases that is spoken in Rayburn meetings is, "Let's find a pathway to yes." The "Pathway to Yes" concept is a lesser-known, but equally important fundamental principle at Rayburn. Board members know very well that Rayburn executives and managers will always strive to take this approach to problem resolution and overall decision-making with positivity and adaptability.

The phrase itself is quintessentially Rayburn, as it is something David Naylor began saying and is now often repeated when corporate-level challenges arise. The phrase resonated deeply when he heard it from Donna Walker, the CEO at Hoosier Energy. He said, "I'm not a fan of the idea that the customer is always right. I know that's the catchphrase, but in our case in particular, we'd rather have open communication about what the customer—in our case, the Member—wants and why. Sometimes there are other ways to solve a problem that they hadn't thought of."

He likened this to a quote often attributed to Henry Ford, "If I had asked people what they wanted, they would have said faster horses." Or Steve Jobs's quote, "Our job is to figure out what they're going to want before they do."

Similar to the popular negotiation phrase "getting to yes," Rayburn's practice of finding a "Pathway to Yes" seeks a collaborative, mutually beneficial solution to problems that impact multiple players. It's a philosophy that focuses on finding a way to satisfy the other party first, especially when the temptation is to simply reject new ideas or demands. It ultimately aims for win-win outcomes, where possible. Sometimes, it doesn't work out, and no has to be no. But the difference is in the attitude with which those conversations are held.

"We seek the pathway to yes, particularly with our Members," said David Naylor. "This gets back to what Rayburn is all about. How do we provide value to our Members when they have a need? In a way, this is just good customer service. When Members have a need, we don't want to come out of the box saying, 'Well, no, we can't do that.' Instead, it's, 'Hey, help us understand what you're wanting. Let's see if we can figure out a solution and try to get to where we're able to provide what you want.' Now obviously there's some caveats to that, but by and large, we try to figure out how can we make things work without compromising our integrity or that of our Member."

This attitude is part of the makeup of any cooperative—to find a way to cooperate. Everyone is aware that whatever the costs of change are, they will get passed down to that metaphorical widow at the end of the line that Rayburn is ever conscious of. But as a cooperative, they are not being driven by a profit motive. They don't have to go to Wall Street or watch their stock prices, so there is some relief from the pressures of purely fiscal concerns.

David Braun elaborated, "We have the ability and mandate to challenge ourselves to look for ways to do things better and with less costs that will add more value to our Members. But nobody is making us do that. We can be fat, dumb, and happy, and never do a thing. In fact, there are a lot of organizations that do that because they really don't care. They just pass their costs down and never try to reduce them. But not Rayburn. Just about everything we do is focused on finding ways to do better."

That positive mindset is a cornerstone of navigating challenges and unlocking opportunities. By maintaining a problem-solving mindset, Rayburn ensures that even in the face of disagreement or conflict, the dialogue remains open to exploring alternatives that lead to mutually beneficial outcomes. It encourages creative thinking and brainstorming, with a willingness to compromise where necessary.

Effective communication is also pivotal in that "Pathway to Yes" attitude, which has enabled Rayburn to build strong relationships with its Members, stakeholders, and the broader community, facilitating agreements that are beneficial for all parties involved. Rayburn's approach transcends the traditional win-lose or zero-sum paradigm of negotiation, using instead a "you before me" approach when possible. This constructive engagement is a testament to the cooperative's commitment to fairness and equity, ensuring that every interaction concludes with respect.

The "Pathway to Yes" is a commitment etched into the very ethos of the cooperative—a commitment to service, to innovation, and to community. This forward-thinking, collaborative approach distinguishes Rayburn in the electric cooperative space because it is in many ways the hardest way to do things in an industry that has historically looked for the easier way. The "Pathway to Yes" is more than a route to agreement; it is a journey toward excellence, reinforcing the cooperative's dedication to fostering positive, lasting relationships with everyone they serve. In doing so, Rayburn proves that a cooperative spirit, coupled with a relentless pursuit of positive outcomes, can indeed turn the most daunting challenges into opportunities for growth and success.

Throughout its history, Rayburn has not only helped illuminate homes but also the lives of those within its communities. Its unwavering dedication to service, to its Members, and to the broader ethos of cooperative principles reflects a culture that transcends transactions, viewing every interaction as an opportunity to build relationships and foster a sense of belonging. Rayburn's journey is marked by moments of challenge and triumph, each step taken with the cooperative spirit as its guide, ensuring that every decision made, and every action taken, aligns with its core values of Integrity, Respect, Excellence, and Innovation. Rayburn's legacy is not just one of providing energy but of empowering lives through community, care, and a relentless drive to do what is right, for today and for generations to come.

CHAPTER 7

WINTER STORM URI

Status Quo is Not Company Policy

DAVID A. NAYLOR

From the Great Dust Bowl to Hurricane Katrina, history is marked by natural events that have profoundly challenged our understanding of the world. These disasters serve as stark reminders of the importance of preparedness. We purchase insurance, cultivate savings, and equip ourselves with first aid kits, all in an effort to safeguard ourselves and our loved ones from the unexpected.

In early February 2021, the small Texas town of Rockwall reveled in the promise of an early spring. National news reports began to indicate the possibility of a storm passing through the southern states, but most Texans went about their business, not paying much attention as a winter weather advisory was issued.

Historically in Texas, winter storms are short-lived—bringing rain, maybe a little ice, and the exceedingly rare dusting of snow. Temperatures might get below freezing for a moment, but never for long. Snow flurries mostly bemuse and even delight Southerners who enjoy the fleeting change of scenery. Most people simply try to avoid driving for a day or two if they can and maybe cover their shrubs and flowers for a few hours. That's about the extent of their concern.

This relaxed attitude can be confusing to northerners who check off deliberate lists of winter tasks when the temperatures drop. Leave the faucets dripping at night, cover the windows with plastic, bring in extra firewood, and wedge an old blanket along the bottom of the door to keep out the draft. If it's going to be really bad, they might even fill the bathtub with water and pull out their flashlights and camp stoves.

Most Texans watched the news with little concern as a destructive storm pummeled the Pacific Northwest. Record-shattering snowfall and freezing rain blanketed Puget Sound, effectively bringing normal life there to a dead stop. However, for the leaders at Rayburn, knowing they were responsible for powering five hundred thousand people across sixteen counties, these news reports were cause for heightened concern. Many factors can impact power facilities and transmission lines, so anytime there is the slightest hint of a potential out-of-the-ordinary weather event, Rayburn follows a lengthy checklist designed to prepare itself.

As stated in chapter 1, Rayburn manages a 1,200-megawatt system with 90 percent of its end users being residential customers. Ensuring a constant and dependable supply involves purchasing electricity in advance based on projected demand. Because the entire electricity generation and delivery system is extremely weather-sensitive, temperatures are a key factor in making decisions about these advanced purchases.

On Friday, February 12, 2021, a winter storm that had been battering the Pacific Northwest turned south and began to head toward Texas. CEO David Naylor and his Executive Team "spent the entire day Friday huddled in a conference room, monitoring projections, assessing our resources, discussing the potential procurement of additional resources and their associated costs, and consulting with the lineman."

As Valentine's Day approached, Rayburn executives carefully considered the supply they thought they would need to keep the power on for their Members. As temperatures continued to drop, Rayburn was 96 percent hedged two weeks prior to Uri, which was considered normal, securing additional resources at real-time market pricing. This established what it would cost to keep the lights on during the storm. Focusing on the core tenet of keeping costs low for its Members, Rayburn believed it had assessed their risks appropriately in the Members' interest considering how the storm was forecast to impact its system. Concerned but not afraid, they left for the weekend, keeping their phones close. The four Rayburn Co-op Members did their best to get the word out to the folks at the end of the line.

Saturday brought more ominous forecasts, but Texans remained largely unfazed. "Big storm coming" and "Prepare yourselves" were the headlines and leading news reports. Store shelves were emptied. The air got brisker. The weekend traffic was light. The weather was getting colder, but there didn't seem to be anything to indicate anyone needed to panic.

On Sunday, February 14, Texans woke to a rare, snow-covered Valentine's Day morning. The few who ventured out discovered that this was more than innocent snow flurries. Everyone cranked up their thermostats and watched as the snow continued to fall. Rayburn Members continued to do their best to inform the consumers on how to deal with the plummeting temperatures.

As the day continued, the true magnitude of Winter Storm Uri became apparent. Record-breaking snowfall and historically low temperatures engulfed the state, leaving roads impassable and driving up power demand as residents sought refuge from the biting cold. Generation facilities began to freeze and fall offline, each having a greater impact on the system as energy needs increased. Rolling blackouts began to impact the whole state and electricity shortages made national news.

By Monday morning, Rayburn found itself grappling with a crisis of unprecedented proportions. Roads were impassable. Gas lines and power generators throughout the state were freezing solid while people stayed home and cranked up their thermostats. The urgent need for electricity to heat structures not accustomed to such freezing conditions spiked demand even further. Considering normal annual temperatures, homes and buildings in Texas are built to get rid of heat, not to hold it in.

Every entity capable of generating power did their dead-level best to generate it, but so much was offline due to the severe weather conditions that it didn't matter. Whether it was with natural gas or wind or solar, power just wasn't available. ERCOT President and CEO Bill Magness posted on social media: "Every grid and every electric company is fighting to restore power right now." Rolling outages were instituted to stave off complete grid failure.

The statewide reduction in energy supply combined with the significant increase in demand meant Rayburn could now only meet 50 percent of the current needs, leading to a staggering predicament. Wholesale electricity prices skyrocketed, hitting the cap of $9,000 per megawatt-hour or $9/kilowatt-hour set by the Public Utility Commission of Texas (PUCT). The normal rate is between $0.02 and $0.04/kilowatt-hour. This caused statewide chaos as the market-dependent energy providers were finding themselves suddenly paying astronomical energy prices on an hourly basis—prices never seen before in Texas.

David Braun recounted that harrowing day, as wholesale power supply invoices piled up at an alarming rate. "When we got that first bill, we said to each other, 'This is not going to work. Let's have them run some projections on what they think the invoice for yesterday and today is going to look like.' It wasn't long before we realized we weren't going to be able to keep ahead of the bills, so we borrowed $150 million in two days from the Cooperative Finance Corporation (CFC)."

To borrow that amount of money in such a short time was unprecedented. The lights started going out all over the state and panic was beginning to creep in as the reality of the situation became clear to everyone. Texas was in the middle of something extraordinary and terrifying, and nobody knew what to do about it.

Rayburn incurred three years' worth of power costs in a five-day period. David Naylor called Clint Vince, the company's primary outside counsel, and said, "Clint, we got a problem. We have bills for over $900 million, and I don't know how we're going to handle this."

Clint said, "Give me thirty minutes and I'll call you back."

Within twenty-four hours, Rayburn assembled a team of experts who recognized the urgency to navigate the crisis. In response to the looming financial disaster, this team charted a course through the tumultuous situation, indicative of Rayburn's resilient and proactive ethos.

Over the coming weeks and months, Rayburn became the first cooperative in the nation to utilize securitization, enabling its Members to spread the payment of $908.2 million over twenty-eight years. In doing so, Rayburn's Members were able to absorb them and amortize them over a thirty-year period without raising the rates for their Members.

Even as Rayburn charted a path toward recovery, the shadow of Winter Storm Uri stretched far beyond the bounds of any single entity. The storm did not discriminate, cutting a swath through the Lone Star State that would be recorded in the annals of history as a dire warning of nature's untamed force. It served as a stark reminder of the vulnerability of our modern systems to the capricious whims of the weather.

TAKEAWAYS

Winter Storm Uri taught valuable lessons. Resilience and preparedness are essential for any organization that wants to thrive in our increasingly unpredictable world. By learning from their own storms, leaders can build stronger, more adaptable organizations.

Comprehensive preparedness is the cornerstone of resilience. Any organization that wants to be prepared for a crisis knows that rigorous risk management and preparedness are of paramount importance. Leaders at Rayburn were not unusual in their focus of meticulously following a comprehensive checklist and keeping a vigilant eye on weather patterns as they braced for the unexpected. They followed best practices by fortifying risk management practices, policies, and structure long before the storm. Then, when it hit, they expanded their internal preparation meetings to include more staff members as a means of ensuring that they could tap into the diverse talent within the organization.

RISK PREPAREDNESS

Often referred to as a regulatory failure, Winter Storm Uri left an indelible mark on Texas, unleashing an economic disaster of unprecedented proportions. The scope of destruction from the storm included loss of life and financial catastrophe in its wake. Its monumental impact is difficult to accurately quantify, but it included possibly hundreds of billions of dollars of damage by the time it finally dissipated ten days later. It was said that the storm cost Texas more money than any other disaster in the state's nearly two-hundred-year history.

In the somber reflection of the storm's aftermath, Rayburn leaders humbly acknowledge that the company's survival is due in large part to the long-established legacy of questioning the status quo. This allowed them to have the foresight to prepare for the unforeseen and to utilize their strengths and agility. This harrowing event became a crucible from which emerged a renewed dedication to resilience and a strengthening of resolve to continue to think critically and to embrace innovative and unusual approaches.

Conducting scenario-based risk assessments long before the storm hit allowed Rayburn to anticipate various extreme weather scenarios and develop contingency plans to mitigate risks. Running through crisis scenarios ensured effective preparation for future challenges.

The strategic use of securitization, a financial instrument as novel to the cooperative world as it was necessary, exemplified Rayburn's unwavering commitment to its Members, a move of unparalleled prudence. It shielded the Members from immediate economic shocks, demonstrating a deep-rooted resilience that would define the co-op's legacy.

Winter Storm Uri also highlighted the necessity of deeply understanding volatile energy market dynamics. Rayburn's reliance on wholesale electricity markets left it vulnerable to sudden price spikes. As a result of lessons learned, Rayburn sought ownership of additional physical generating assets to help control and limit its exposure to the energy market. The acquisition of the natural gas power plant, Rayburn Energy Station, in 2023 and the expansion of its Power Supply Department were strategic moves to augment their wholesale power function for its Members. This symbolized a concrete step toward energy independence and self-sufficiency. With this, Rayburn not only shielded itself from the volatile winds of the wholesale electricity market but also illuminated a path for others in the sector, demonstrating the merit of asset ownership over reliance on market forces. The company infused its operations with robust versatility, ensuring its commitment to its Members and to operational sustainability.

FINANCIAL RESILIENCE

Financial resilience is paramount for business continuity in any size company and any industry. Establishing partnerships or networks with reliable resources ensures agility in adapting to unforeseen challenges. For Rayburn, securing a $150 million loan from the Cooperative Finance Corporation during the crisis showcased the company's ability to act swiftly and decisively. It also showed that Rayburn's strong relationships with its business partners, cultivated over time, were strategically important. Building financial resilience meant maintaining healthy cash reserves and establishing lines of credit or access to emergency funding.

The underlying strategy reveals the profound importance of cultivating enduring partnerships and the foresight to establish robust financial safeguards. It's about more than just knowing where to turn to secure emergency funding; it's about fostering trust with financial partners long before a crisis hits. This approach, when implemented consistently, transforms relationships from transactional dealings to strategic assets.

No matter the industry, companies can aim to create a financial buffer that can absorb the shocks of sudden market shifts or operational disruptions. This could involve strategies such as diversifying revenue streams, renegotiating terms with suppliers to reduce immediate financial strain, or investing in flexible assets that can be liquidated in a pinch.

Rayburn's response to the storm underscores the necessity for comprehensive risk assessments that account for a variety of disaster scenarios, including those that may seem improbable. A proactive stance on risk management, incorporating both financial and operational resilience planning, can ensure a company's stability and its ability to deliver on promises to customers in the most tumultuous times. It's about understanding the full spectrum of your company's risk exposure and having a layered strategy to manage it—from insurance and capital reserves to flexible operational capabilities.

This includes strengthening supply chain resilience. Diversifying suppliers and building redundancy in critical supply chains is as essential as assessing vulnerabilities and transforming potential weaknesses into strengths that minimized risks to our operations.

In practice, building financial resilience means regular reviews of capital structure, maintaining open lines of communication with financial institutions, and staying informed about new financial instruments that can provide quick liquidity. It also means integrating financial stability into the company's culture, ensuring that all levels of the organization understand the role of fiscal responsibility in long-term sustainability.

Businesses of any scale can start by conducting a financial health check, identifying potential vulnerabilities, and creating actionable plans that enhance their financial fortitude. These steps form the bedrock of resilience, enabling companies to not only survive unexpected events but to emerge with their integrity and operational capacity intact. An often-overlooked step in financial resilience is to work on fully funding the trust bank not only within the organization but also outside of it. In many instances, the recovery from a crisis requires the assistance of vendors, lenders, and advisors. Keeping those relationships strong can lead to greater recovery and resilience.

CRISIS MANAGEMENT

In times of unprecedented crises like Winter Storm Uri, effective crisis management was indispensable. Rayburn rapidly assembled a multidisciplinary team, including legal, economic, and financial experts, to astutely tackle the challenges head-on. Having a comprehensive response plan in place was crucial. As business leaders, Rayburn's executive leadership team had to be prepared to act decisively and mobilize resources to address unforeseen challenges. This readiness to quickly rally a diverse team underlines a key lesson for businesses everywhere: in crisis lies the opportunity for unity, innovation, and transformation.

Effective crisis management is more than the assembly of a capable team. It requires a long-established culture that promotes rapid decision-making and autonomous action. Just as an electrical grid relies on the seamless cooperation of its components to distribute power, so too must a company's leadership synchronize to navigate business upheavals.

Leaders wanting to build organizational resilience must have an intimate understanding of their organizational assets and their people, where the collective knowledge and experience of the team can be leveraged to make informed, strategic decisions at a moment's notice. This, along with a robust crisis plan, can give companies the edge they need to not only withstand the unforeseen but also emerge with new strengths, primed for future challenges.

REGULATORY COMPLIANCE AND ADVOCACY

Winter Storm Uri exposed regulatory shortcomings in Texas that exacerbated the crisis. In the aftermath of the crisis, Rayburn has taken an active role in advocating for robust regulatory frameworks and reform of inadequate rules. Winter Storm Uri highlighted the importance of maintaining compliance with regulatory requirements as an essential element in maintaining stability in critical industries like energy.

One of the reasons Rayburn emerged not just as a survivor but as a standard-bearer for change was that it advocated for itself with the lawmakers and decision-makers who oversaw their regulations. Rather than waiting for a solution to present itself, the company found ways to create and promote fortified regulatory structures that promised greater resilience and reliability.

Rayburn's advocacy in the legislative arena is reflective of their commitment to not just weather the storms but to reinforce the entire structure against future tempests.

This forward momentum is emblematic of a larger imperative for all critical industries: to transform regulatory compliance from a checklist to a cornerstone. It is about ensuring that rules and regulations evolve in tandem with technological advancements, market shifts, and environmental challenges, shaping an infrastructure that is both stable and dynamic.

LEARNING FROM FAILURE

Winter Storm Uri provided Rayburn with valuable lessons. Analyzing the root causes of the crisis and implementing corrective measures has better prepared Rayburn for future challenges. Fostering a culture of continuous learning and adaptation was crucial for navigating uncertain business environments effectively.

The path Rayburn charted post-Uri now serves as an example of turning adversity into an advantage, proving that an open-minded corporate culture can convert challenges into stepping stones toward greater corporate strength and stability.

Readiness and resilience are not just reactive measures but proactive business strategies that transcend industry boundaries. They underscore the importance for any business to establish and nurture a culture where learning is iterative and constant, where risk is not just managed but strategically anticipated, and where change is embraced not as a disruption but as an opportunity for growth. It's this forward-thinking and systemic approach to crisis management and business operations that can provide invaluable insights for organizations aiming to bolster their resilience in an unpredictable world.

Leaders improve and strengthen their companies when they treat setbacks as informative experiences. Conducting thorough analyses to understand what went wrong helps identify areas for improvement. By fostering a transparent culture where mistakes are openly discussed without fear of blame, organizations encourage learning and innovation. This approach allows for the adjustment of strategies, reinforces risk management, and promotes a culture of resilience, thereby turning past failures into lessons for future success.

Organizations can use setbacks as a vital part of the learning journey by incorporating these eight steps into their crisis management plan:

1. Promote the Growth Mindset: When an organizational culture perceives failure as a springboard for growth, teams are encouraged to experiment, take calculated risks, and understand that setbacks are often the precursor to innovation.

2. Conduct Post-Mortem Analyses: After a failure, analyze what went wrong without assigning blame. This allows teams to dissect the failure to understand its root causes and avoid repeating the same mistakes.

3. Welcome Feedback: Create mechanisms for feedback at all levels, including open lines of communication where employees can report issues without fear of retribution.

4. Invest in Your People: Use failure as an opportunity to identify skill gaps and invest in training and development. Equip teams with the knowledge and tools they need to overcome challenges more effectively.

5. Set Up Resilience Planning: Develop resilience strategies that prepare your organization for future setbacks. This involves planning for various scenarios and having contingency plans in place.

6. Document Lessons Learned: Maintain a repository of lessons learned from past failures. This serves as a valuable resource for training new employees and for teams to reference when facing new challenges.

7. Celebrate Effort: Recognize and reward the effort and learning that come from failed attempts, not just the successes.

8. Revise Policies and Processes: Consistently update organizational policies and processes to reflect what you learn. This helps to institutionalize needed changes and prevents the recurrence of similar issues.

By treating failure as an integral part of the learning curve, organizations can foster resilience, encourage a more innovative mindset among their workforce, and ultimately turn potential negatives into powerful positives.

TRUE LEADERSHIP

Leadership is as much about fostering trust and confidence as it is about decision-making and strategy. During Winter Storm Uri,

Rayburn's leadership team exemplified this by not only adapting to rapidly changing situations but also by ensuring that every team member was equipped to handle the emerging challenges. They did so by embracing a two-pronged approach.

First, they practiced what can be called "responsive leadership"— a commitment to quickly respond to new information and situations as they arose. This responsiveness was not limited to the top echelons of management but was encouraged at all levels, creating a nimble and empowered workforce capable of localized decision-making. Leaders were accessible, providing clear and actionable guidance that helped maintain operational continuity despite the crisis.

Secondly, Rayburn invested in the human element of leadership. Rayburn prioritized open communication and transparency with employees, believing that keeping employees informed and engaged was essential to ensuring their well-being and fostering a sense of support and belonging within the organization at a time when there was uncertainty. To achieve this, Rayburn regularly updated employees on the status of or changes to operations or policies related to the storm. They encouraged employees to voice their concerns and contribute solutions.

By prioritizing open communication and transparency, Rayburn ensured that employees felt supported, valued, and empowered to navigate challenges together as a unified team. Recognizing that a crisis can be as much a psychological battle as a physical or economic one, leaders established regular check-ins with staff, not only to update them on operational matters but to gauge and respond to their well-being.

The robustness of Rayburn's leadership during this period was not a product of coincidence but rather the result of deliberate strategic leadership development that prioritized adaptability and empathetic communication. As a result, Rayburn emerged not just intact from the storm but with a workforce that was more cohesive, resilient, **and** committed to the company's vision than ever before.

CHAPTER 8

BOLDLY LOOKING AHEAD

*This recognition validates our commitment to our employees
and reinforces our mission to make a positive impact
on our Members and the communities we serve.*

DAVID A. NAYLOR

From its inception as a modest paper G&T through the transformative journey of NERC compliance, Rayburn is now a significant infrastructure owner. This path was neither easy nor simple, especially while trying to maintain an emphasis on operational excellence. Long-time outside legal counselor, Clint Vince reflected on the company's expansion, its strategic positioning, and the visionary approach of its leaders.

> When I first started representing Rayburn shortly after
> they were organized by Ray Raymond, the one thing that
> always attracted me was just the character of the leaders
> that I was dealing with. They were salt-of-the-earth,
> decent leaders who cared about their community and
> their customers. In their case, their customers are their

Members, which is very unusual. But that's the model of an electric cooperative. They were a little tiny operation on a dirt road.

And now if you fast forward, it's extraordinary. It has a beautiful campus serving some of the fastest-growing areas of the country, especially for co-ops. This small operation was created based on Raymond's instinct to get away from the South Texas nuclear project. The break-off co-op he started has turned into a major utility. They've gone from just contracting for power and services to a utility that now owns its own power plants, transmission lines, and substations. It's an amazing growth story.

Through it all, Rayburn hasn't lost the integrity of its leadership. They're amazing because they're very smart, very experienced, and have great judgment. I'm really impressed with the quality of people they hire. They are strategic, capable, and calm. It's been fun to watch them grow their team from what was really a mom-and-pop operation to a serious multi-billion dollar business. And they continue to use that momentum to keep getting better.

Even though this was not their goal, this little Texan G&T is becoming a pioneering force in the energy sector, setting a standard for being innovative and adaptive in a swiftly changing energy environment. The Rayburn culture has proven itself through crisis, as Winter Storm Uri showed. When other companies faltered, Rayburn avoided organizational fragmentation by investing heavily in their people and staying focused on lofty (seemingly unreachable) goals. They embrace the challenge in alignment with what former IBM CEO Ginni Rometty said, "Growth and comfort never coexist."

Rayburn's future is anchored in its foundational values that have propelled its growth. Its strategic evolution has been underscored by significant milestones, including overcoming financial adversities, embracing technological advancements, and expanding infrastructure. All of this is built on a commitment to Integrity, Respect, Excellence, and Innovation and serves as a beacon of inspiration for what lies ahead. Rayburn remains at the forefront of the energy industry's evolution, ready to face new challenges with the same tenacity and vision that have always been its hallmark.

Rapidly increasing demand and technology advancements continue to reshape the energy industry landscape, and yet, within this very maelstrom, it has carved a resolute path. By continuously challenging the status quo, Rayburn ensures every step taken is a stride toward efficiency and growth engineered to meet the demands of tomorrow.

LEGACY OF INNOVATION

Innovation at Rayburn has become tradition. The profound heritage of ingenuity has enabled the company to not just keep pace with the rapidly evolving energy sector but to lead and redefine it.

Rayburn's commitment to maintaining its innovative edge in the face of shifting energy landscapes is evident in its strategic embrace of new technologies and markets. When market failures and regulatory challenges arise, the company responds not with resistance but with resourcefulness, turning challenges into opportunities for growth and learning.

The strategies Rayburn has adopted over the years, including the unique wholesale power contract structure and the acquisition of Freestone Energy Center and later Rayburn Energy Station, are testaments to its adaptability and strategic thinking. It's a system designed for adaptability, ensuring that Rayburn can provide stable and affordable power to its Members regardless of market volatility. Decisions are made not just for the cooperative's benefit but for its Members' needs first.

As Rayburn looks ahead, it plans to continue its legacy of innovation. As Board member John Ed Shinpaugh said:

> Change for the sake of change is bad. Tradition for the sake of tradition is bad. You have to respect both and use them accordingly. You can't just sit and watch business. You have to live it and breathe it and be a part of it. You have to become a student of your own industry and your core business. You have to have a tenacious appetite to leave no stone unturned and to use what you find if it's best for your organization. This is what Rayburn does very well. David Naylor doesn't put parameters or shackles on how his staff can interact with each other or us, the Board of Directors, who are, on paper, David's boss. You've seen organizations where the upper management wants to shield everyone or control the messages that go out. That's not the Rayburn way. This flat organization works very well, especially in this atmosphere where you don't have an option but to grow and change. It's like walking through a maze blindfolded right now.

There are monumental changes on the horizon for the energy sector and seismic shifts in the power needs that the United States is going to have. Rayburn is not just preparing for disruption; it is actively planning for—and in some cases, instigating—disruption. By staying ahead of the curve, they know that when the energy market shifts, they will not just be ready, they will be at the forefront, leading the charge.

At the heart of everything is the company's dedication to service excellence. As Rayburn grows, it has not only scaled its operations but has done so in a way that maintains its connection to the community it serves.

With its eyes set firmly on the horizon, Rayburn is charting a course for sustained growth and continued excellence, driven by the cooperative values that have powered its journey from the very beginning. Rayburn's growth narrative is not merely about expansion but about enhancing the service quality and efficiency for its Members. Every strategic move has shown that it is not merely responding to the needs of the present but is actively shaping the future of energy service delivery. Continuing investment in generation within the ERCOT market represents Rayburn's proactive approach to not only securing its energy future but also to positioning itself as a leader in operational excellence.

This commitment to innovation is a part of Rayburn's DNA, and it will continue to be a driving force as it carries the torch into the future, ready to light the way for the energy industry.

CULTIVATING TALENT AND LEADERSHIP

It's one thing to attract talent and another entirely to keep it. People quit their jobs for various reasons, many of which are due to poor management. In other words, people usually quit people, not jobs. Inadequate support, lack of recognition, or a toxic management style can lead to employee dissatisfaction and eventual departure. If an employee feels stagnant in their role and sees no opportunities for advancement or professional development, they may decide to seek employment elsewhere. When employees feel undervalued and their contributions go unrecognized, they may seek appreciation elsewhere. Or a mismatch between an employee's values and the company's culture can lead to discontentment and a decision to leave.

People want to feel like they matter. That they are contributing in an important way to something greater than themselves. At Rayburn, the wisdom of talking to people smarter than oneself is not just practiced; it's a strategic imperative. Here, leaders routinely engage with and hire individuals whose expertise exceeds their own. This habit has become a cornerstone of Rayburn's culture. They strive to always be ahead of the curve, ready to embrace change and address future challenges with the most informed and capable team possible.

One of the newest staff members, Marc Cantrell said:

> It's very different than what I knew before on the commercial side of the industry. I traded for a long time. A trade floor is as competitive as any place in the world. You are trying to kill it to reach this goal, and you're also trying to outdo this guy who might be your friend. Boy, you want to outdo him every day. Group A has to destroy Group B because we have to get our bonuses. That kind of thing.
>
> That attitude doesn't exist at Rayburn. Here we are serving our Members, so we do the best job we can for them. That's the goal. This creates more of a team, a community culture, than if you're just out chasing the bottom line. You're not shooting to hit a budget number for profit this month, driven entirely by the dollars. You just want to get the job done and do things the right way. It's very value-driven.

> This is an exploding company. The growth is logarithmic, but at the same time, due to its age, there is stability there. Rayburn treats us so well. There is no financial gain to the way they take care of people, so the direct benefit is the quality of life they provide to us as staff members. Rayburn sees a return in happy employees, not a bottom-line return. It would be so much easier to follow the industry and do what everyone else is doing. But that's not what they do here. They put their money where their mouth is, so to speak.

Rayburn's strategy for talent development is two-pronged: it combines the structured rigor of formal training programs with the flexibility of informal learning experiences. For example, the Breakfast Club initiative emerged from an intrinsic culture of challenging the status quo. This focused, ongoing leadership training program identifies high-potential staff members and provides them with the tools and knowledge to realize their full potential. It exemplifies Rayburn's commitment to nurturing its talent pool, providing an avenue for employees to learn about communication, company culture, agility, decision-making, and team resilience. The success of this initiative has proven that investing in people leads to a more robust and innovative organization.

Through additional initiatives like education reimbursement and cross-departmental collaboration, employees are encouraged to grow both professionally and personally. The close-knit, family-like culture is not just an internal feel-good factor; it's a strategic asset. The cooperative has weathered crisis after crisis because it can pull together as a community.

By managing culture with as much dedication as it manages business operations, Rayburn has created an environment where employees are empowered, leadership is cultivated, and integrity is non-negotiable. The cooperative's strategic focus on human development has not only contributed to its success but has also ensured that as Rayburn grows, it retains the essence of what has made it a trusted and innovative force in the energy market.

CULTIVATING A RESILIENT AND ADAPTIVE CULTURE

In a world where change is the only constant, Rayburn is committed to fostering a resilient and adaptive workforce in the face of a rapidly transforming industry and unpredictable challenges.

The flat organizational structure is more than a strategic design—it's a deliberate choice that fosters transparency, accelerates decision-making, and nurtures a sense of family among employees where every individual is seen, heard, and valued. It has helped create an environment where cultivating talent and leadership is not just encouraged but expected, as the cooperative prepares to meet the future with a workforce that's as resilient as it is skilled.

Rayburn's culture thrives on challenge, seeing it not as a hurdle but as an opportunity to grow stronger and more cohesive. It's a culture that understands that the true measure of resilience is not just in withstanding challenges but in emerging from them more united and focused than before. The cooperative's resilience was put to the test during Winter Storm Uri, as it disrupted power supplies across Texas. Rayburn's response was not just about restoring power but also about upholding a commitment to serve and protect the community. The company's strategic approach to power supply and its ability to swiftly adapt to market changes reflects a culture that does not shy away from challenges but meets them head-on with determination and ingenuity.

In cultivating this resilient and adaptive culture, Rayburn assures that it is not just prepared for the future but is actively creating it, with a workforce and leadership poised to innovate and excel in the face of any challenge.

FACING FUTURE CHALLENGES

Rayburn has long understood that the future is a tapestry woven from the threads of past experiences, current actions, and strategic planning. In an industry as dynamic and vital as energy, the horizon is always dotted with challenges that demand both attention and innovation. Strategic planning includes anticipating the widespread impact of electric vehicles on the grid, for example, ensuring that infrastructure and policy evolve in tandem to support this clean energy transition.

This proactive approach extends to navigating the intricacies of regulatory and market complexities. Rayburn's focus remains unchanged: to secure a sustainable future for its Members without burdening them with undue costs. It's an approach that balances fiscal responsibility with the unwavering pursuit of innovative solutions.

As Rayburn looks to the future, it is not with trepidation but with a clear-eyed view of the challenges ahead. The legacy will no doubt be one of enduring impact built on the cooperative's foundational values of Integrity, Respect, Excellence, and Innovation.

Expansion and growth have been hallmarks of Rayburn's journey, particularly in the Texas region, where its forward-thinking strategy has seen it grow in influence and capability. Here, the long-term vision is expansive yet precise with employees not just as workers but as architects of the future, equipped with the skills, knowledge, and drive to forge new paths in the energy industry. Rayburn seeks to be remembered not just for the power it provided but for the paths it paved—for its Members, for its employees, and for the communities it serves.

If Rayburn had taken a different direction at any critical juncture, the company would have undoubtedly looked significantly different. For example, it could have allowed the status quo to be good enough for its Members. Instead, it acquired the Rayburn Energy Station and expanded its energy portfolio, adding 758 megawatts of natural gas-based generation to its assets and pushing its assets to over $1 billion, an investment that not only enhances the cooperative's capacity, it also strengthens its independence from power purchase contracts, contributing to a more secure electricity supply for the future. Because they held true to their core values and refused to accept the status quo, Rayburn has emerged as one of the most desirable places to work in Dallas, the fourth-largest city in North America.

THE *DALLAS MORNING NEWS* RECOGNIZES RAYBURN ELECTRIC COOPERATIVE AMONG THE TOP WORKPLACES IN DALLAS-FORT WORTH FOR 2023

Ranked #5 for Small Business Category, #1 Overall for Best Benefits

In 2023, it was recognized as one of the Top Workplaces in Dallas-Fort Worth for 2023 by *The Dallas Morning News*. Specifically, Rayburn ranked #1 for Best Benefits overall in the Special Awards Category and #5 in the Small Business Category out of 187 similarly sized companies. David Naylor said, "At Rayburn, we consider our greatest strength to be our dedicated and talented team. This recognition validates our commitment to our employees and reinforces our mission to make a positive impact on our Members and the communities we serve."

The recognition is based on a survey of over 166,000 employees at nearly six thousand nominated companies in Dallas-Fort Worth. Being recognized among the top workplaces in Dallas-Fort Worth by *The Dallas Morning News* confirms Rayburn's reputation and prestige within the business community. This recognition not only acknowledges the company's success but also highlights the commitment to its foundation.

In a region known for attracting major companies and corporate investments, being selected signifies that Rayburn is among the top businesses in an area that consistently ranks high for attracting new companies and business projects, showcasing its strength and appeal within the market.

This is but one more benchmark in the journey of vast potential that lies ahead. Rayburn's story is about innovation, strategic foresight, and an unwavering commitment to community. It includes enduring relationships, empowered lives, and industry standards elevated. The legacy Rayburn wishes to leave is clear—a legacy of Integrity, Respect, Excellence, and Innovation, all leading to service that transcends the daily business of keeping the lights on.

CONCLUSION

Since 1979, Rayburn Electric Cooperative has been a paragon of adaptability and innovation. It serves as proof that in times of upheaval, organizations anchored to a steadfast ethical foundation can thrive while perpetually evolving. In both good times and bad, companies that enforce strong core values are the ones that make it through. Rayburn is a great example of how to get ready for change before it hits. They invested in creating a resilient workforce, which gave them the flexibility to handle recent challenges that took down less prepared competitors.

In an industry often resistant to move away from tried-and-true methods, Rayburn continues to reshape the Texas energy landscape. By staying true to its foundation, it has written a story not of conformity but of audacious ingenuity, unwavering tenacity, and a firm commitment to transcend the ordinary.

The world is changing so fast that it is crucial for leaders to stay alert and be ready. The pace of progress cannot outpace the pace of your company's innovation. There are abundant opportunities for those who dare to imagine and adapt.

Rayburn is a mosaic of determination, relationships, insight, courage, trust, and forward-thinking leadership. Here, adaptation is not merely a survival tactic but a strategic imperative because leaders know the heart beats strongest in those who can harness the power of change. Their unwavering commitment to empowering employees has unlocked innovation to learn, to innovate, and to boldly usher in an era where electric cooperatives are not just participants but custodians of a brighter, more sustainable future. Its motto that "Status Quo is Not Company Policy" has enabled this nimble co-op to rapidly scale its vision to national prominence.

This book is an invitation to those who stand at the edge of a decision with a mix of trepidation and excitement. The hope is that it will be a source of inspiration for all those who seek to rewrite the script of their own organizations. Follow the Rayburn way and you can also emerge as a trailblazer. May this narrative kindle the spirit of innovation. May it be a steady guide through transformation. And may you, like Rayburn, create a legacy that will endure in your own industry's history of what can be achieved when Integrity, Respect, Excellence, and Innovation converge.

ABOUT THE AUTHORS

HEIDI SCOTT

Heidi Scott has worked in the nonprofit, private, academic, and federal sectors since 2000. Home-based in Texas, not far from the Rayburn Electric Cooperative headquarters, she regularly travels around the world as a professional writer, ghostwriter, and editor. She has a BA and MA in English from Colorado State University and has written over thirty books, including a handful of best-selling titles.

Outside of word engineering, Heidi fosters a pathological curiosity to see new things, meet new people, and embrace new opportunities. Her ancestry includes French pirates, Danish Vikings, and American pioneers, which might explain some of her life choices. She and her husband are happily passing along a hunger for adventure and a desire to do hard things onto their four children, who currently live in three different states.

DAVID NAYLOR

David A. Naylor is the President and CEO of Rayburn Electric Cooperative, a generation and transmission cooperative serving four distribution cooperatives who serve across sixteen counties in northeast Texas.

David has over twenty-five years of experience in the utility industry beginning with C. H. Guernsey & Company where he served as a managing consultant for Rayburn. David's leadership, expertise, and innovation resulted in him first joining Rayburn as the Executive Vice President and then becoming its current President and CEO. He is a licensed Professional Engineer, with a BS degree in Electrical Engineering from the University of Oklahoma. As a resident of Rockwall, David plays an active role in serving as a community leader and stakeholder.